My Humorous Japan

BRIAN W. POWLE

NHK出版

My Humorous Japan

Introduction

Do you enjoy a joke or perhaps laughing at life itself? Do you want to better your English without reading a lot of dull textbooks? If the answer is 'yes' to both these questions then this little book is for you.

First let me tell you something about it. It's made up from the collected stories from the NHK Radio Eigo Kaiwa magazine. Many readers wrote to me suggesting it might be a good idea to put them together in book form so here it is. In fact, I would like to thank my loyal readers for their cheerful and encouraging letters over the past years. As their ideas are more useful than mine concerning the use of the book, I'd like to quote a few sentences from these letters.

One reader wrote, "The stories are about the same situations that I myself have been in : the rush hour on the Yamanote Line, skiing, staying in a ryokan, trouble with the neighbours and many others. It's interesting to read a foreigner's opinion about them. I like to laugh at them too."

Another reader wrote, "I was surprised that I could read these stories without a dictionary. The short simple sentences in modern English make them easy to understand. The cartoons are funny and make the stories even easier to understand. I am more sure and confident of my English ability than I was before."

Well, I hope this book will help you in the same

way that it has helped these two readers. They say that a picture is worth a thousand words. I don't know about that. However modern research has shown that cartoons of a humorous nature plus a text using everyday words give both pleasure and education. That really is the aim of the book.

How can you use the book? One reader told me that he looked at the cartoons. He tried to guess the plot of the story just from the cartoons. He then read the story and looked at the cartoons again. In this way he could see whether his guess had been right and of course he could get the full meaning of the story.

Are you going abroad or do you have any foreign friends or business acquaintances? Then why not use the book or the material in it to get their point of view on these different situations? You'll always have a ready source of conversation at your finger-tips.

Finally, I must ask you to excuse, sometimes, my type of humour. British humour does tend to be a bit critical, pointing out weaknesses here and there. I think in Japanese you call it 'hiniku'. Still, I think the British and Japanese sense of humour are very similar. We enjoy laughing at ourselves without being angry. Life would be dull if we only enjoyed 'the sweet'. We should laugh at 'the sour' too. Anyway, I hope that whether you find the stories sweet, sour, strange or unusual, you won't find them dull. I also hope that you can enjoy a good laugh and improve your English at the same time.

Contents

The Daily Fight on Japanese Trains

Most of us spend a lot of time in trains. I know I do. When I go out to the Hon Atsugi campus of Aoyama Gakuin, I spend at least three hours in trains on the Odakyu Line and Inokashira Line. During the early morning rush hour, it's quite a fight even to get into the train. Some time ago my sister wrote me a letter in which she described a television programme about Japan she had seen on British television. She remembered one scene very well. It was a scene where strong railwaymen were pushing arms, legs and people into a train so that the doors could shut. The Tokyo train was so crowded. Then she added, "I can't believe this REALLY happens. They were only doing it for the BBC to make the programme more dramatic." I wrote and told her I had to enjoy this "drama" every morning. It's the survival of the fittest!

Actually, some people wonder why

Japanese are so strong in the world today. Japanese live longest, enjoy good health and are the wealthiest. I know the answer. It's because Japanese minds and bodies are trained to be strong and competitive from childhood in trains! Maybe the kindergarten student who fights off others for a train seat will be the president of a big company one day. Even weak-looking old Japanese grandmothers can compete with the best. I remember one little old lady waiting on the platform of Shibuya station. She was waiting in line just in front of me. She looked so weak I wondered whether I should help her into the train. However, when the doors opened, she took off like a guided missile

The old lady took off like a guided missile.

throwing her bag on to the empty seats. If there had been a "Train Olympics", she would have got a gold medal. I'm sure that racing for seats keeps her fit and that she'll live to be a hundred.

Actually, it's very important to have a happy or cheerful attitude in Japanese trains. At first, I used to get very angry when people trod on my feet, put their

Surrounded by 'noise monsters' in the early morning.

elbows in my face, or pushed my lower back with their hands. I used to get even more angry when they were just silent and never said, "Excuse me" or "I'm sorry". In London you always apologize for such actions. Then I understood I was being very foolish. You push people so many times, perhaps 500 times in the course of 5 minutes so it's quite impossible to keep saying "I'm sorry" 500 times! Now I silently pull, push, squeeze and trample with the best of them! Instead of putting up my blood pressure by being angry, I actually enjoy it. You can even see me smile while silently engaged in these violent acrobatic actions which help keep me fit without paying a yen. And if I get the

9

extra bonus of obtaining a seat, so much the better.

Of course, I have to admit there are certain "train monsters" who do make me angry. There are boys with long hair who listen to rock music over headphones. In the early morning when one is very sensitive to even a slight noise on trains, the unpleasant, tinny, jangling noise that comes through these headphones, is very irritating. I can't read my newspaper properly. Then there are groups of two or three gossipping schoolgirls. They shout at each other in such loud voices. It seems they want the whole train to hear their intimate personal news. A soft voice used to be considered a polite tradition for a girl. But not now. They say that Japanese girls are now getting stronger than men. I think so. I know it must be true just by listening to their voices on trains!

Of course the "sleeping tanuki" student is well known. He's usually a strong boy with a short haircut, the member-of-a-sports-club type. He will never give up his seat even if the old lady standing in front of him is dying of a heart attack. He seems to be in a deep sleep. "Seems" is the key word here because he's actually pretending so as to avoid giving up his seat. In addition, he usually opens his legs wide over the seat so he's taking up

The method of getting a seat from a 'sleeping tanuki'.

the space for two people. Actually, this kind of train monster doesn't worry me. I say "sumimasen" in a loud voice accompanied by a strong chopping motion of the hand to show that I mean to sit down and nothing will stop me. Then with an equally strong vigourous motion of the hips I squeeze myself down into the seat. Even train monster has to move up and close his legs in the face of this kind of attack.

A new kind of monster is the seat reserver. About a month ago I saw a girl leave her handbag on a seat space while the train was waiting in Shibuya station. When anybody tried to sit down, she would say. "I'm sorry. I'm keeping this seat for my friend." Finally one old man wasn't buying this argument. He told the girl, "What do you think this is? It's not a theatre where you can reserve seats." He then picked up the girl's bag and placed it on her knees before sitting down. Good for him. That's the way to deal with seat monsters!

Aunt Mabel's Search for the REAL JAPAN

Some people don't look very favourably on elderly Japanese when they visit Paris. On being asked whether they would like to try some of the famous French cooking cuisine, they might reply, "No thank you. We'd like sushi or tempura." In a way I can understand their choice. Elderly people like the things they know best.

I found this out when an elderly aunt of mine visited Japan some years ago. In her letter she wrote that she didn't care about the usual tourist sites. She wanted to see the REAL Japan. She wanted to see the REAL Japanese and how they REALLY lived. With this in mind, I reserved two rooms at a typ-

Aunt Mabel's idea of THE REAL JAPAN

Aunt Mabel BEFORE and AFTER she entered a Japanese train.

ical ryokan in Nikko.

She duly arrived and told me that she was staying at a Ginza 5-star hotel. Except for the high prices, it was NOT her idea of the real Japan. Only in Japan can you pay $15 for coffee and a sandwich!

Anyway, I called on her the next day. We went on a very crowded subway to Asakusa station. I told her it would be easier to take a taxi. She refused saying, "I want to be with the real Japanese people in Japanese trains." She soon discovered how real they were when she was being crushed by millions of real Japanese in the train.

At first Aunt Mabel, for that was her name, was delighted with the Nikko ryokan. "Oh, it's so artistic. I could almost imagine Madame Butterfly committing hara kiri on the atami, I mean the tatami." However, this temporary feeling of happiness didn't last long. She was soon in my room wearing the wrong slippers on the sacred tatami. I could see she wanted to complain about something. But first I had to give her a little lecture. I said, "When you come in, you have to take off your street shoes and put on slippers. You take the slippers off again when you enter the room. You walk on tatami with bare feet. Then you must wear special slippers for the toilet. You put the original slippers on again when you walk down the passage to my room and then you must take them off again when you enter it!" She said she understood and that it was better than doing acrobatic exercises.

She then launched into her complaint. "Where is the toilet? I've searched for it high and low and I can't find it." Rather fatuously, I told her it was low as I showed her the toilet in my room. She looked at the

Those are the WRONG slippers, Aunt Mabel.

elevated hole in the floor with dismay. "But ... how ... how ... do I use that?" I told her that she could be shown how to master basic arts such as the tea ceremony, flower arranging and even sumo wrestling. Then I added, "But you'll just have to work out how to use a Japanese toilet for yourself. Anyway, I'll give you some advice. Just imagine you're a girl guide looking for something on the ground." Looking somewhat puzzled by this helpful advice she returned to her room.

After unpacking I went to her room. She then told me she'd also been looking for the bathroom. I then explained more mysteries about public bathing in ryokans. She didn't like the idea at all. She then asked if men would use the same bath. As we were in the country, I replied, "I don't think so, but there MIGHT be some men in there." Hearing this, she refused to go down. "How could I go into a bath where men might see me naked? What would my husband, your Uncle Albert, say?" Actually, he wouldn't have worried because Aunt Mabel doesn't have the kind of figure which attracts male attention. Finally, I said, "You haven't seen the REAL Japan unless you've experienced a public bath." That did it. With the air of a kamikaze pilot about to make his final dive, she entered the bathroom. There was just one last problem. She looked at the small towel and remarked, "This is just a washcloth for my face. Where is the bath towel?" When I told her that the small towel was used both for her face and her body, she was very surprised. "That's how REAL Japanese dry themselves after a REAL Japanese bath," I told her. In fact, it did seem rather a small piece of cloth to dry the rather large areas of Aunt Mabel's skin. By this time, it was evident that she was not too eager to experience any more of the REAL Japan.

It seemed the Nikko ryokan visit would be a disaster. It was not. Aunt Mable loved the ofuro. She enjoyed the tempura and sukiyaki dinner and aquired an immediate taste for sake. As we were leaving her room dressed in kimonos, we saw some country geisha going into a room where a party was being held. "Oh, I'd just love to go to a real geisha party." I told her she could not go to it until she was a real Japanese geisha. With a sigh of sorrow she said, "What a pity. I'm too old for that now. If I were younger, I would become a Japanese citizen. Then I'd study to be a REAL Japanese geisha."

Britain and America Are Divided by English!

In Japan there is a kind of undeclared language war. As you may have guessed, it's between British and American English. Of course being British myself, I feel there is only ONE kind of English and that MUST come from England! Naturally American teachers think differently.

Of course, the two versions of the English language must sometimes be very difficult for Japanese students. British and Americans may have quite different words for the same object. One year students may have a British teacher who tells them 'a flat' is a place where you live. The next year, if they have an American teacher, she may say, "No,

A language problem for Japanese.

that's wrong. You live in an apartment not a flat. A flat means that you have no air in your tire." Yes, it's difficult. Which is right? I guess you have to change your English according to whether you're in England or America or according to who is giving the examination.

In one sense British English is more polite. For instance if a British person needs a match, he may ask, "Excuse me, I wonder if you would kindly lend me a match to light my cigarette please." This would be too long for Americans who might just say, "Gotta light?" Of course the last version is shorter and easier. Perhaps, that might be one reason why Japanese sometimes prefer American English.

Yet in another sense, American English could be said to be more polite. This is especially true over sentences and words concerning death and toilets. The words "toilet" and "lavatory" frequently used in England, sound rude to American ears. They prefer "rest room" or "comfort station". I remember one time I was in Bronx Zoo, New York. I had a rather urgent call of nature so I asked a man where the toilet was. He looked very surprised. He replied, "Can't you find it? Why, it's signposted all the way. Look over there." I told him there were only

An Englishman's problems in New York

signs to "comfort stations." He looked at me as I were quite mad and said, "But those ARE toilets." Naturally British people would be equally surprised if you asked the whereabouts of a comfort room or station. Generally, if a lady wants to use a toilet she may ask to powder her nose. A man may ask to wash his hands or use the bathroom. This should be generally understood on both sides of the Atlantic. However, in certain places in Britain, this may still cause some misunderstanding. It's best in this case to be direct by just saying, "Where is the toilet?" Otherwise you may be directed to a room where you can ONLY powder your nose or ONLY wash your hands!

Dying or passing on

Now, to change the subject, Americans use a more indirect vocabulary on matters concerning death. Perhaps they consider this to be a rather unpleasnt subject so that is why they use softer sounding words than the British. Let me give you an example of this. A British person might say, "Mr. Smith died yesterday. His body has already been placed in a coffin. He will be buried in St. John's cemetry tomorrow." However an American might say, "Mr. Smith passed on yesterday. The loved one is resting in a casket. He will be interred in St. John's Memorial Gardens tomorrow." If you compare the wording of these two speeches you will see they are quite different. But the meaning is the same. I suppose Americans find such words as "died", "coffin", "buried", "body" and "cemetry" rather distasteful.

Similarly, other words are also disguised.

A maid becomes "a domestic helper". A toilet cleaner becomes "a sanitary engineer", a salesman "a business representative" and so on. When a stockbroker tells you that you are losing money you are informed that you have "a negative cash flow". Frankly I don't know whether American English is more polite than British English. But I believe in calling a spade a spade and NOT an agricultural implement!

Now let's have a test. Without looking at the answers can you guess which word is American and which word is British in the following pairs of words?

①pavement ( ) sidewalk ( )
②cookies ( ) biscuits ( )
③drapes ( ) curtains ( )
④lift ( ) elevator ( )
⑤holiday ( ) vacation ( )
⑥gasoline ( ) petrol ( )
⑦pictures ( ) movies ( )
⑧chemist's ( ) drugstore ( )
⑨(bank) cheque ( ) check ( )
⑩programme ( ) program ( )

Now here are the answers ... and I hope you didn't look at them!

①pavement (B)　sidewalk (A)
②cookies (A)　biscuits (B)
③drapes (A)　curtains (B)
④lift (B)　elevator (A)
⑤holiday (B)　vacation (A)
⑥gasoline (A)　petrol (B)
⑦pictures (B)　movies (A)
⑧chemist's (B)　drugstore (A)
⑨cheque (B)　check (A)
⑩programme (B)　program (A)

　Well, how did you do?　Very well?　Congratulations!

About Tokyo
Noise Pollution

I think if you rent a house in Tokyo like me, you are certain to have some difficulties. I know I did when I rented a house in Shinjuku. My problem was noise pollution. From six in the morning until midnight there was some kind of sound or another to disturb my peace. Let me tell you about it.

For a start there was my American neighbour. Originally, he studied in Paris to be an opera singer. But he ended up by teaching in an English conversation school. However, he couldn't forget his opera and used to practice his singing from six in the morning. To begin with I would hear, "La..la..la...la" with his notes getting higher and higher. This would

6 a.m.—Operatic arias

25

always wake me up instead of an alarm clock but the alarm clock would have been better! After he had practiced his notes twenty times, he would then go on to operatic arias from Carmen or Aida. By this time I was quite awake. When I mentioned his singing to him, he replied, "But doesn't it move your heart to hear the Egyptian Prince singing of his love for the imprisoned Ethiopian Princess?" I said, "Yes, but not at six in the morning. And besides, you are not an Egyptian Prince and I am not an Ethiopian Princess!" I don't think he liked my practical way of thinking.

Then the opera attracted further noise. My landlady or house owner Mrs. Abe made

7 a.m.—callisthenics musical exercises

no secret that she hated opera in general and my neighbour's arias in particular. As a kind of revenge for being woken up by 'The Bullfighter's Song' from Carmen, she would turn up her television to full volume! This resulted in callisthenics music competing against the Bullfighter's Chorus for mastery of sound. And my bedroom was in the middle of it all!

But Mrs. Abe was not finished yet with disturbing the peace. She would then go through a noisy gargling and spitting ritual. Of course you gargle with water when you have a sore throat and then you spit it out. Indeed this can be done quite silently. But when done by Mrs. Abe, it sounded like the San Fransisco earthquake followed by the sound of an elephant being thrown into a swimming pool. Of course, there's no doubt that she must have had a continual sore throat. That was because I could hear her shouting and screaming at her poor husband. Most of us only have sore throats during the winter but hers lasted the whole year round because of this. Of course her husband often used to come home drunk but really I couldn't blame him.

By this time it would be eight o'clock. I would then make a cup of coffee and enjoy it in the living room. But I could not enjoy

8 a.m.—engine warming plus carbon monoxide

my coffee in peace. I have to say when I first rented the house it was situated in a beautiful garden. When I returned to Tokyo after a summer holiday, the garden had been turned into a parking lot! It was very sad but one has to face facts. A parking lot is more profitable than a garden. But while Mrs. Abe got the money, I received all the noise and all the pollution. And so it was that the noise of a car having its engine 'warmed up' disturbed my peaceful coffee break. Like the opera singer next door, the car's engine grew louder and louder. The smell of poisonous carbon monoxide gas could be detected in my living room. And still my enemy, that horrible car did not move. Finally, I could not suffer it any more. I went out and above the noise, I shouted at the driver, "Can't you move your car and warm up your engine on the road outside."

He replied that he couldn't because it might hurt his car's engine. I told him he was hurting my human body with all his poisonous gas. After all I had only ONE body. He could easily get another engine. He answered by blowing cigarette smoke in my face. Usually I am really a very gentle person. But at that moment I wished I had a bottle of very strong acid to pour over the body of his expensive foreign car. Instead I locked the gate of the parking lot so he had to get out and unlock it again.

Well, I could go on about other noises:the karaoke enka singer, the sound of a thousand cats meowing their love songs at midnight, the student piano player 'murdering' pieces by Chopin and a pile driver used for repairing the road outside...and like my house owner's gargling, the repairs seemed to go on throughout the whole year! With all these complaints, you must think I'm a very miserable person...but don't take me too seriously. I'm only joking!

Secrets of Success
at Viking Buffets

Many years ago, I remember being very puzzled when one of my girl students told me, "I'm going to enjoy a Viking next Sunday." She was equally surprised when I replied, "Oh, you mean you're going to see your boyfriend from Sweden or Denmark?" Of course I didn't know at that time that "Viking" was the term that Japanese use for a buffet help-yourself-to-all-you-can-eat meal. In England we only think of a Viking as one of those invaders of Britain who used to wear helmets decorated with horns. They say that the buffet style of meal was first introduced by a Scandinavian airline at a famous Tokyo hotel. Hence the name Viking.

I'm going to enjoy a Viking

Well, whatever the name, buffets are now extremely popular here. They are both reasonably priced yet they give you the feeling of enjoying a luxurious banquet or feast. When you are hungry, it is a wonderful sight to see all that wonderful food heaped in various dishes on one long table. And Japanese chefs arrange it so artistically that they can make even quite cheap food look expensive. In fact most Japanese food is a delight to the eye as well as the stomach. I think if Picasso had seen a beautiful "Kaiseki Ryori" he would have been influenced into a new form of art.

Anyway, the full enjoyment of a buffet is an art in itself. One of my Japanese friends says he takes his family once a month on a Sunday to a Tokyo hotel buffet. He has four growing children with appetites to match. His advice is to get to the hotel early. "Be sure to be the first in line as the door opens," he says. As soon as the doors open, his children do an Olympic sprint to get the best table. But it won't be the table from which you can get a lovely view of Tokyo near a window. It will be a table from which you can get a lovely view of the buffet! My friend says his food and his wife's shopping bills at supermarkets are huge. In fact, I personally know these bills would be enough to feed twenty families in a third world, developing country. So when his chidren are eating so much at home, he says, "Eat slowly, Don't make pigs of yourselves. No, you cannot have a second helping. You are already too fat as it is." However, just this one time a month, his children are allowed to make pigs of themselves. He even smiles indulgently as little Masataka returns for the tenth time from the buffet with a heaped plate. He also says if you are at the buffet from the beginning, the food is still fresh. It's not so good if it's been stewing for a long time even if it is in a silver dish.

Little Masataka making a pig of himself

I have also learned from experts that buffets contain both cheap and expensive food. This is certainly true at business parties in hotels. Naturally, the expert at "buffetmanship" wants to get the best food for himself. He does it as soon as possible before it is gone. You will find his plate heaped with lobster, smoked salmon, shrimps, roast beef and other expensive goodies. Others may just have to be happy with leftover chicken in brown gravy, meatballs and vegetables! After the expert has raided the table, the smoked salmon and lobster plates are quite empty except for some decorative vegetables. How does he do it? I'm afraid he's a rather greedy and unpleasant person. For example, as soon as he sees a waiter bringing in the salmon and lobster, he goes straight to it like a guided missile. It may be that somebody is just in front of him about to take the last piece of roast beef from the plate. However, buffet expert's fork will suddenly come up from behind, spear the meat and put it on his plate faster than the speed of sound! It's almost like a conjuring trick. It also may be that when you are talking with buffet expert, that he will suddenly excuse himself

Buffet expert in action

by saying, "Oh, excuse me please. I see my old friend Professor Ikeda over there. I have to discuss the theory in his new book about sea and marine life. Goodbye!" Actually, there is no such person as Professor Ikeda. The only sea and marine life which he's interested in, is the fresh lobster which has been placed on the buffet table! And he's not going to let social conversation get in his way.

At one hotel buffet, the headwaiter noticed two students go up to the buffet 12 times. Yet they didn't seem to be eating much. Where was all that food going? Soon they got up and started leaving the restaurant. One of them was carrying a big cello. Suddenly the cello case accidentally broke open and all the food which the students had hidden came tumbling out on to the floor! The students were very ashamed.

They said they wanted to hold a party but had no money to buy food.

After reading these stories I hope you don't think that Mr. Powle is a greedy buffet expert. Even a mouse wouldn't be happy with the small amounts he eats.

Japanese Parties Are Fun

I must say I really enjoy Japanese parties. Even the most serious people become relaxed and do silly things. I've seen a company president stand on a table with a paper hat on his head sing a silly song. Students who are so quiet in the classroom, suddenly relax at a nomiya party. Suddenly, they can speak English much better than in a classroom. The fact that you can spread out on tatami makes for a more relaxed atmosphere than you find in western parties

Of course, funny things can happen. I remember some time ago a friend invited me to his wedding. Unfortunately I got delayed because my taxi got stuck in a traffic jam. When I arrived, all the guests had gone into the wedding hall. To make matters worse, they could not find the place where I was supposed to be seated. Well, they found a place for me anyway. Suddenly, the music of Wagner's Wedding March could be heard.

I leaned forward to get a view of my good friend Shuji and his beautiful bride Atsuko as they entered the room. But quite a different bridal couple appeared! I didn't know them

Quite a different bridal couple appeared!

at all. I didn't know what to do. So I told the Master of Ceremonies. I apologized and asked to be excused. But he wouldn't hear of it. He said, "We hope you will stay. Please make a speech. If you don't mind, you can tell our guests what happened." Then he asked to see my invitation card. "Oh, your invitation is for NEXT week," he said. Anyway, I stayed and made my speech. Everybody laughed. I guess it was not only at the funny incident but at my funny Japanese also.

Another time I arrived a bit early for a wedding ceremony at a Christian chapel in Roppongi. I made sure it was the right date this time. While I was waiting, I was very surprised when a priest approached me and asked, "Would you mind giving a bride away?" In fact I was so surprised I couldn't say anything. So the priest repeated his request. He explained, "You see a young American couple want to get married. As the bride's father isn't here, we asked the American ambassador to give the bride away in his place. It seems at the last moment he can't make it." Well, I obliged. Actually the bride was so pretty I didn't really want to give her away! It was a very simple ceremony lasting about 15 minutes. Quite a contrast to my Japanese friend's ceremony which lasted over an hour with choirs, sermons and all the trimmings.

I did NOT expect a fish-head for breakfast!

Another time I went to Shimizu where a welfare organization was giving a New Year's breakfast party. Prominent in the food spread before me was a great big fish head! When I commented that it made an interesting decoration, my neighbour told me, "It's not a decoration. You have to eat it." The eye of the fish seemed to be looking at me as if challenging me

The fish head seemed to be following me.

to eat it. But I couldn't so after leaving the table, I left it on the plate. Soon a waitress came running after me with the fish head, "You've forgotten this. I'll wrap it up for you so you can take it to Tokyo." Out of politeness I didn't like to refuse. As I had some time before the train went, I went into a coffee shop. I left the fish head under the seat. I had just got past the cashier when again a waitress came running up with my fish head. Again she said, "You've forgotten this." So I took the Shinkansen leaving my beautifully wrapped fish head on the seat. Once AGAIN a railwayman came running up with it in his hand. I think he was surprised at my angry look as he said, "You've forgotten this." Anyway, it wasn't wasted. At that time I had a Siamese cat called Nikki. She enjoyed the fish head very much!

A Skiing Trip
in Hokkaido

I'd like to tell about my first experience of skiing. I really didn't want to start. I thought I was too old to begin such an energetic sport. But a professor and some students persuaded me that, "it's easy." Actually, it was not, as I found out.

Niseko in Hokkaido was the chosen place for my skiing debut. We hired a car in Sapporo to get there. After many hours of driving we arrived at a very lonely-looking place. It might have been in the middle of Siberia. Of course, this was many years ago. It is probably different now.

We checked into a rather primitive min-shuku. The dinner was delicious. The beef was cooked over a Genghis Khan style barbecue. We washed it down with plenty of hot sake and whisky, though not together of course. In fact, I was in quite a good mood until I tried to go to sleep. There were ten of us sleeping on the floor of an 8-mat room!

We were packed in like sardines.

We were literally packed into that small space like sardines are packed into a can! The boy behind me kept kicking my head with his feet. I guess he was dreaming that he was a star in a football game! A man next to me was snoring so loudly, it was enough to wake up the dead. Added to that, was the noise of a noisy mahjong game going on next door. You could hear it clearly through the wafer-thin walls.

Well, at last I managed to get to sleep ... but not for long! I was soon woken up at 6 a. m. by my neighbours, the noisy mahjong players, rushing down the stairs near our room. It wasn't long before they were doing their noisy physical exercises just below our window. "Hum .. hee .. ho .... hum ... hee ... ho," they shouted as they stretched themselves. As you can imagine, I wasn't very happy by this time. But I was comforted by the thought of my "western style breakfast" which was being cooked especially for me. This consisted of bacon and eggs alright .... but they had been cooked the night

Ordeal by noise : mahjong chips, snoring and exercises!

before and left in the ice box all night! It was quite a fight to cut up the cold hard eggs and cold greasy bacon. The professor asked if it was delicious. With a brave smile I told him it was but that I would prefer a Japanese-style breakfast the next day.

I was told that Niseko snow was the best in Japan. I wished the same could have been said for the hotels at that time. Anyway, an unfortunate instructor was asked to teach me skiing. I say "unfortunate" because she didn't know what a difficult student she had!

In a sense, skiing is worse than scuba diving in the early stages. It LOOKS easy but it isn't. Even putting on the old-style boots and skis was difficult and tiring. Modern equipment which just springs into place, is much easier to handle. Then came the actual business of learning to ski itself. I won't go into the painful details of all the times I fell down and all my mistakes. My instructor, Miss Ando didn't know much English. She knew a few sentences. I suppose she thought that if she shouted them often and loudly enough, they might have some positive effect. I can hear her even now. "Keep your stomach in." "Your hips are all wrong." (I didn't know how to make my hips right.) "Bend your knees." "Shoulders back." Well, I made no progress after two painful lessons. I know she must have been a

I couldn't please my severe teacher.

good teacher and I'm sure I was a terrible student. Anyway, I decided to go off on my own. I never like anybody watching me when I keep falling down. I practiced a bit on a very gentle slope. After two days I was quite proud of myself. I could ski without falling down for five minutes on end . . . . even if my hips were still all wrong.

On the third day I even dared to take the chair lift to the top of the first slope. And it was here that I met with an accident. I was standing at the top of the slope just meditating on how I would manage the difficult journey down. Then it seemed that a rock or even an avalanche hit me from behind. It had the impact of an express train. There I lay almost buried in snow. If you've ever been skiing you know the feeling. You daren't move because you're sure you've broken every bone in your body. At last, I was aware that somebody was trying to help me to my feet. It was a strong-looking student who kept saying "Sumimasen. Sumimasen." Then I understood that it was HE who had hit me from behind. At last I was standing up. To my amazement, nothing was broken. With a last "Sumimasen", he was about to ski away. But I soon stopped him. I ordered him in angry tones, "Get my skis. Now put them on. My ski sticks are

over there. Get them." I guess he was surprised because kindly Japanese are quick to
accept an apology. I suppose he'd never met
an angry red-faced gaijin before! Then he
confessed that he was a member of the noisy
mahjong-playing group in the room next to
ours! That made me even more angry. By
the time I was finished, the poor boy looked
as if he were ready to commit hara-kiri.

Well, dear readers, you must be tired of all
my complaints. The story has a happy end-
ing. The apologetic student invited me to
join his friends in the next room for a little
sake party. We had a very good time singing
and swapping jokes. Finally the student
asked me, "Will you forgive us? We'll be
very quiet and careful on the ski slopes in
future." I replied, "Of course I do. I'm sorry
I was so rude to you in the first place." As
Shakespeare said, "All's well that ends well."

The "Girl Shortage" Is a Problem for Japanese Men!

Life was not so pleasant for a girl who lived in Japan a hundred years ago. Her only hope was to marry as quickly as possible and pray that she would be born as a boy in her next life. An unmarried daughter of mature years was not welcome in any family in those days. Let us take an example. We'll call her Etsuko for the purpose of this story. She lived a hundred years ago and has just had her third omiai meeting. In a sense, according to her mother's thinking, it has been successful. The man has at last agreed to marry Etsuko. Already her mother is talking about marriage plans. Then Etsuko says, "It's just impossible. He's old enough to be my father. He has bad skin and bad breath. I can never love him and never marry him. I'd rather commit suicide."

At first her mother is at a loss for words. Then she angrily says, "You will obey us and you WILL marry him. Marriage is the most important thing in your life. Love is not. Love will come later."

After this conversation, it is likely that "traditional Etsuko" will be condemned to a loveless marriage. In fact love didn't come later. Etsuko was bullied by a cold-hearted husband. And when he was absent, she was treated like a slave by a tyrannical mother-in-law. Naturally, many of these traditional marriages were very happy indeed. But unfortunately many girls used to suffer as Etsuko did.

However, the situation is quite different for modern Etsuko. She can pick and choose. The trouble, is, that so many men want to marry Etsuko that she can't make

Modern Etsuko can pick and choose her type.

up her mind. What kind of a boy does she really like? Sometimes it's the athletic sportsman type. Soon she gets tired of him and prefers the scholastic type. It's fun reading his poetry and foreign books. She also likes music-playing, gift-giving and car-owning boys. Others bring her flowers and want to play tennis. She just can't make up her mind which to choose!

How is it that modern Etsuko has such a wide choice compared with her traditional counterpart of sixty years ago? For one thing, it is estimated that there are 400,000 more boys than girls of marriageable age nowadays. Therefore according to the laws of supply and demand girls are a more attractive 'product' than boys. Secondly, girls can go out and earn their own living. Many of them make more money than boys these days. They are not dependent on men for every yen. For instance OLs (office ladies) enjoy dining out together in expensive restaurants, shopping and even travelling to exotic places like London, Paris or New York. Why should they be burdened down with a husband and children at an early age? Let's get back to modern Etsuko. Her mother was very angry with her for rejecting a very nice boy from a wealthy family, who graduated from a top univer-

It's Etsuko's 'measuring test'.

sity and had a brilliant career before him in a large and famous trading company. Her mother asked, "Why did you reject him?" Etsuko replied, "He didn't pass my measuring test." When asked what this test was, Etsuko replied, "I measured him to see how tall he was. He just wasn't tall enough. I could never wear my Italian high-heeled shoes when walking out with him! Also I learned that his trading company was cutting down old and valuable trees in Sarawak." Etsuko's mother just couldn't understand such foolish reasons for rejecting a husband. All she could say was, "Well, Diana is much taller than Prince Charles." Naturally Etsuko replied, "Yes, but Tadashi is NOT Prince Charles." After that her mother was silent because she couldn't think of a suitable reply to that remark.

Of course, some girls are finding out that

marriage just does not suit them at all. They'd prefer to be career women who can reach the top of their professions. Actually, there are not so many top lady executives in Japan as in Europe or the States at this time. But they are getting there. Quite a lot of hotel owners, graphic designers, advertising executives and company directors are ladies these days. Perhaps this dynamic type of lady would like to enjoy "the role reversal system". What's that? This means that the wife is the breadwinner of the family. It's she who goes out to work while her husband stays at home to do the cleaning, cooking and look after the children. This role reversal system seems to work very well in advanced countries such as Denmark and Sweden. Japan may be too conservative for such an idea at the moment but it may be acceptable in the future.

The role reversal system.

Anyway, the fact

remains that the marriage situation is getting more difficult for men. One man I know, Hiroshi, has been rejected five times! He's in despair. He's been on a diet to make himself smart and slender. He's changed his glasses to contact lenses. He spends twice as much on cosmetics as his sister to try and make himself handsome. But for him the answer is always "NO". Now he even hates the thought of another "omiai" meeting. He says he'd rather fight Saddam Hussein in Iraq! What can he do? Perhaps he could go to "Hanamuko Gakko". This is a special school which helps men to become more desirable in a future bride's eyes. At the end of the course he can get a certificate which states that he's "A Model Man". But does a bride want "a Model Man"? Like the words in an old song she might say, "I love you just the way you are."

My Zen Experience
Was Hard but Wonderful

The early samurai were really strong men. In fact, they would be called 'the strong silent type' nowadays. They could even face death calmly without worrying. We can see this is true from the story of the 47 ronin in Chushingura. But present-day Japanese worry quite a lot over small things. They worry about exams, politics, the consumption tax, health, old age etc. etc. And I know I worry more than most people. But isn't it stupid?

Why can't we be like the old samurai and have calm, peaceful minds?

We can. We can do it through zen meditation. I tried it once and it's an experience I shall never forget. I'd like to tell you about it.

Many years ago, I was writing for the Asahi Evening News. One time the editor asked me to go and interview the high priest of a famous Buddhist zen temple in Kamakura. However, when I arrived at the temple, I was very surprised. A priest told me, "Yes, we are expecting you. We understand that you want to spend the night and study zen meditation!" The editor's secretary had made some mistake. Anyway, I couldn't interview the high priest because he was away in Kyoto. So making the best of the situation, I said, "Well, as I can't have the interview, I'll be happy to spend the night doing zen meditation."

But the severe-looking priest didn't seem very happy at my words. He then said, "No, you can't come. You are not serious. We do not welcome foreigners who just come to study zen out of curiosity. It's better that you go back to Tokyo." This seemed to be a kind of challenge to me. I said that I had come all the way to Kamakura to learn about zen so I was not going back. "Alright", said the priest, "But you must do EVERYTHING just the same as a Japanese person." I agreed.

I was shown how to sit correctly in the zazen position. I was told that breathing was important. It should be slow and shallow. I asked, "Should I think about one hand clapping?" The priest said a lot of foreigners asked that question. But it was best to keep my mind as calm and empty as possible.

I kept thinking about a hamburger

"I don't think that will be difficult for you," he said. Perhaps he thought my mind was always empty anyway!

After receiving his instructions, I was allowed to enter the meditation hall. I felt very strange. It was as if I had stepped into a scene in Kyoto five hundred years ago. On either side of the great hall, there were lines of still and silent figures meditating. In fact I could only see them after a few minutes. My eyes had to get used to the dark. Only the distant sound of a clock ticking could be heard.

Zazen was not so difficult for me. Even though it was in the middle of winter, I didn't feel a bit cold. I had one problem: I

..., but it kept sliding back onto the floor.

couldn't keep my mind empty. I had come without eating so I was very hungry. I kept thinking about a hamburger with lots of french fried potatoes! Eventually, the hamburger went out of my mind. As I followed the instructions about breathing and *zazen*, I felt really happy and peaceful. I could feel all the muscles of my body slowly relaxing. Not only did the visions of a hamburger disappear but all my worries seemed to go away too. They say if your brain waves reach an alpha state, you can feel very peaceful. Perhaps that is what happened. Of course zen philosophy is very deep and difficult to understand. And yet it can be very simple at the same time. All I can say, is, that I had a very wonderful feeling while I was doing *zazen*.

When it was around 1 a.m., we were allowed to have three hours sleep on a rather hard *futon*. At 4 a.m. somebody rang a little silver bell. Everybody jumped up. With one throw, they threw their *futons* onto a shelf against the wall.... except me. My *futon* kept sliding back onto the floor. The young priest watched me severely. How I hated that *futon*! All my calm thoughts disappeared. I kept throwing it up on the shelf and it kept coming down! At last after watching me severely for awhile, the priest did it for me.

Then I had another problem. After a rather simple breakfast, one of the senior priests gave us a very long lecture about zen thinking. We all had to sit in the 'seiza' position while we listened. Well, it was very difficult for me because my legs started hurting and aching so much. So I sat in the *zazen* position. After all, my legs were under the table so I thought nobody could see

The seiza position was very difficult for me.

them. But the severe young priest did! He immediately told me to get back into the *seiza* position again. The kind senior priest suggested that as I was a foreigner, I might be allowed to sit in the *zazen* position. But the severe one replied, "No. He said he would do EVERYTHING the same as a Japanese person." He then translated it into English in case I hadn't understood it the first time. Thirty minutes later when I tried to stand up, I just fell down on the *tatami*. My legs seemed to be made of butter. Anyway, my zen experience was a wonderful one. I shall never forget it.

A "Sweet and Sour" Stay in Kyoto

When I first went to Kyoto it did not seem to be a friendly place. It seemed that the people were very cold. In fact I was sorry I had taken the long and expensive journey from Tokyo just to see Kyoto. In the end I changed my mind. Now I like Kyoto and its people very much. Anyway, let me tell you about my first visit.

As soon as I arrived in Kyoto I went straight to the travel information office in the station. It seemed to have been started especially for foreign tourists so I thought I would have no problems. But I was wrong. I told the travel information officer that as I was in Japan I wanted to stay at a Japanese inn. To my surprise he replied, "But as you are a WESTERNER, you should stay at a WESTERN hotel."

He then continued, "You have to eat raw fish and sleep on the floor!" But I was not going to be put off. I said, "I WANT to eat

Difficulties at the travel information office.

raw fish. I WANT to sleep on the floor. Now get on the phone and book me into a ryokan." He looked at me as if I were quite mad and started his round of telephone calls.

Even in those far off days I could understand a bit of Japanese. His calls to the hotels were phrased something like this. "We have a strange foreign tourist here. He insists on staying in a ryokan. Do you have a room for him?" After five such calls which ended up with five refusals of "No, we haven't", I became a bit angry.

"Just tell them a visitor wants a room. That's all. Do NOT tell them I'm a FOREIGN tourist." I said. After a few protests he agreed to do that. Of course he got a room for me with the first call. He gave me a slip of paper on which he'd written the name and address of the hotel. It also confirmed that the room had been reserved in my name.

He was kind enough to see me to a taxi and tell the driver the directions to the hotel. After a few minutes drive, the taxi stopped outside the gate of a very charming ryokan. It was real "Kyoto style". One of my few Japanese expressions at this time was "Gomen kudasai". This I shouted very loudly rather in the manner of Aladin shouting "Open sesame" at the entrance to the treasure cave. At last a little old white-haired lady came on the scene. I think at first she didn't see me properly because she was bowing all the time. But when she did, her eyes seemed to open up in a combination of shock and terror. Indeed it probably was a severe case of "Gai-jin Shokku". In spite of her advanced years she ran away surprisingly quickly. Even if I'd been a man from Mars, I don't think I could have surprised her

I might have been a man from Mars.

more.

After a long wait of about ten minutes, a teenage boy at last appeared. He waited for me to speak but I was silent. At last some words of broken English came out of his mouth, "No stay here. No like. No speak English. Goodbye."

Actually, I was very angry and wanted to shout at him. But luckily I reminded myself I was in Kyoto. Like many foreigners first coming to Japan, I had read up a bit about Zen Buddhism. So with what I imagined to be Zen-like calm I answered. "Here is my reservation slip in Japanese. The name of your hotel is there. I sleep HERE." The boy examined the slip for a long time. Perhaps he felt it would contain some information to make me go away. In the meantime I said "I stay HERE. Only here. Let's go." Then in a very strong way I took off my shoes. I picked up my suitcase and said, "Show me to my room please."

At first the boy, scratching his head didn't know what to do. At last a lady who must have been listening to our non-productive dialogue behind a screen came forth. With many bows and "sumimasens" she led me to a very nice room with tatami and a view of a lovely little garden. She apologized for my cold reception.

My Japanese improved with sake.

"You see we are worried for you. We have never had a foreign guest before. You know our way of sleeping, eating, taking a bath and using a toilet is so different from what you are accustomed to."

I replied, "That's why I'm here."

In the end my ryokan visit was a great success. Over dinner I spoke with the lady and her shy son. After three tokkuri of sake my Japanese seemed to improve greatly. Then as they relaxed, their English became more fluent. After a two-night stay there we parted the very best of friends. They admitted at first they thought I was a rough and rude foreigner. In a way I suppose I was. But sometimes it's necessary to be cruel to be kind. As I was leaving the lady said, "Now we have international sense. Come again." I now think Kyoto people are very nice once you get to know them.

Television Viewers See the Summit of Mount Everest

30% of TV viewers in the Kanto area watched the first live pictures from the Summit of Mount Everest. But some of them were angry because it interrupted a baseball game between the Yomiuri Giants and Hanshin Tigers!

Actually, it was a very historic occasion. Climbers from Japan, Nepal and China met at the summit ... for their own 'summit conference.' They had climbed up two different sides of the world's highest mountain which is 8,848 meters high. They overcame many dangers and hardships including extreme cold. The temperature is 35 degrees below zero Centigrade! One climber poured a

TV viewers see Mount Everest.

bottle of whiskey on to the ground. He said it was to remember and honor climbers who had died trying to climb the mountain. One of them was Hidetaka Mizukoshi who died of heart failure the previous month.

Some local people in Nepal couldn't believe that so many foreigners would make so much effort just to climb a mountain. They were sure they were looking for treasure and jewels. However, television told them the real story. Said Ram Thapa, "I could now see with my own eyes that they were just climbing in the spirit of adventure." Actually, this Sunday Mr. Powle is going to climb a summit. He's going by elevator to the 'summit' of a big Tokyo hotel to enjoy a Sunday buffet! It's not so exciting as Mount Everest but it's safer.

One sunny day, some passengers in a plane of a commercial airline were traveling at an altitude of 7,200 meters. It's quite high though not as high as Mount Everest. They were sitting comfortably in their seats on their way to Hawaii. Suddenly, six meters of roof was torn off by the wind! Right in the plane they could see the blue skies of Hawaii for the first time! In fact, at such a height most of the passengers thought it would be the last thing they would see. They didn't expect to stay alive ... but they did. The clever

A surprise view of the sky.

pilot landed the plane safely. Some passengers were hurt and an air hostess was missing. Perhaps she had been blown into the sky by the wind. Why did this accident happen? The plane was 19 years old and had had 89,000 landings. Maybe it was just too old.

Well, Kiyoharu Saito was not too old to do his job ... which was cracking or breaking into safes. A safe is a strong iron box in which money and valuables are kept. Saito was arrested after cracking a safe of the Kumamoto Bus Company and stealing ¥140,000. Of course, the police asked him many questions. Finally he told them, "I've cracked 800 safes in less than two years in every prefecture except Okinawa!" The police couldn't believe that one man could crack so many safes in such a short time. But it was true. So far they have found 743 cases of burglary probably carried out by Saito. He stole more than ¥34 million usually from hospitals and schools. They don't always look after their money so carefully!

The high value of the yen is attracting many imports and some of these 'imports' are not so good. In fact, they are men similar to Mr. Saito. One of these men is Mr. Philippe Jamin. He confessed that he and his gang stole five valuable paintings from a Paris art gallery. They were by the famous French artist Jean Corot. He thought he

"We'll reserve this picture for Japan."

could get more money for them in Japan than elsewhere. While in Tokyo, he did not waste his time. He also took part in the ¥300 million robbery of a bank security van according to his confession. In a sense he is similar to a man who tried to sell a violin by the famous violin maker Stradivarius. It had been stolen from a New York musical instrument dealer. Like Mr. Jamin, he thought the theft of the violin would not be known in Tokyo and that he could get a higher price for it. After his arrest, he knew he was wrong. Of course I think Japan should import more, especially Scotch whiskey... but not stolen paintings and violins or the people who steal them!

New Yorkers
Like Japanese Lifestyle

We all know that Americans enjoy buying Japanese cars and electronic goods. But did you know that many young Americans are also enjoying a Japanese lifestyle too? That's right. Yuppies (Young Urban Professionals) who are rich, young and intelligent people eat lots of tofu and sushi. They say it's much more healthy and delicious than their fastfoods such as hamburgers, hot dogs and fried chicken. In this picture you see a typical yuppy couple in their one-room apart-

Japanese lifestyle in Manhattan.

ment in Manhattan. They are saving space by using a futon. Nichola, a popular model, is bringing some sushi to her husband. Although she has many beautiful

clothes, she likes to
wear monpei and
kasuri at home.
"They're so warm,
cheap and com-
fortable." she says.
They also have an
Akita dog called
Yasu who goes jog-
ging in Central

Yoshimi helps starving Africans

Park with them. When Yasu barks, he says
"Wan . . . wan, wan . . . wan." This is
Japanese. American dogs usually say,
"Bow . . . wow, bow . . . wow." By the way,
the man in the picture is called John. He
works for a Japanese television manufac-
turer near New York. Where do they export
their televisions? To Japan of course!

However Japanese ideas are not only
popular in New York. Although it's not so
well known, Japanese are doing a lot of
good in Africa too. In picture A, we see some
starving Africans in Ethiopia receiving par-
cels full of food. Actually, sending food and
money to Africa is not a good idea. Often
the money gets lost. When the food is fin-

71

ished there is no more. Once again the Africans may go hungry and starve. Actually Yoshimi Saito aged 28 has a much better idea than the government. You can see him in Picture B. He is showing African natives how they can help themselves. He is showing them how they can get little streams of precious water from a lake under the ground. With water they can grow corn and rice. With corn and rice, they can raise many animals. They never have to go hungry again. They say that things in Africa will be very bad again this year. Japan and other developed countries should be sending young experts like Yoshimi Saito to Africa . . . but not food and money!

They say that a picture is worth a thousand words. In fact thousands of years ago, almost all teaching was done with the help of pictures. Later because of the use of words, pictures were not utilized any more. Now, however, modern educators are going back to pictures again. Pictures are being used more and more in 'new education.' Even a very famous financial paper is using cartoons to explain difficult money matters to businessmen! Why are pictures so good for education? Of course we all enjoy looking at pictures which help the learning process. But this is not the whole reason. Experts tell us that

The best way to remember English words

our brain is divided into a left section and a right section. The left section processes words and numbers in a business-like way. The right section is more 'artistic' and emotional. It handles pictures, feelings and emotions. For example if you look up the word 'cheese' in your dictionary, you may soon forget it. If you see a picture of a piece of cheese with the word, you will remember it better. However if you see a mouse eating the cheese you will remember it best. That's why we have pictures with my stories. You can use both the left and right sections of your brain, so I hope you can remember them better. Actually, this is a good exercise. Just look at my pictures ONLY. Then see how much of the text you can remember.

Anyway, Mariko will always remember her Valentine's Day. In fact, at the beginning of February she was wondering about her Valentine Day's gifts. She thought she would send some chocolates to her English teacher Mr. Ikeda. She always enjoyed his classes. Maybe, it was because he was young, handsome and had a nice smile. She was happy to buy some expensive chocolates and send them to the teachers' boarding house where Mr. Ikeda lived. After February 14, she was waiting for Mr. Ikeda's nice smile as he said, "Thank you" to her. He said nothing. She was very disappointed. However, later in the day, Mr. Honda wanted to speak to her. He was fat, with very little hair and not at all handsome. He was the German teacher and for some reason Mariko did not like German so much. She was very surprised when Mr. Honda said, "Thank you, my dear. Thank you so much. I enjoyed eating the Valentine's Day chocolates you sent me. You're so kind." Yes, she was VERY surprised. She went to see Mrs. Suzuki, the teachers' boarding house mother. "What happened?" she asked.

Mariko's surprise Valentine

Mrs. Suzuki replied, "Well, you see Mr. Ikeda had so M A N Y Valentine's Day presents. Poor Mr. Honda had NONE at all. He was so unhappy that I decided to give your chocolates to him. I'm sorry." Actually, Mariko was such a kind girl, she didn't mind. Later, Mr. Honda was so kind to her, that she came to enjoy German. In 1989 she will give more chocolates to Mr. Honda!

Midori Goto Is the Heroine of a U.S. Textbook

Why is teenager Midori Goto a heroine? Why will young people all over America want to follow her example? It's because her story will appear in a U.S. textbook called 'On The Horizon.' It features people who have shown great bravery and courage under very difficult conditions.

When Midori was only 14 years old she was very good at playing the violin. In fact she was so good that she was asked to play as a solo violinist with the Boston Symphony Orchestra. I'm afraid my cartoon is not quite right as it is difficult to fit in a symphony orchestra in such a small space! Anyway, right in the middle of the concert her violin string broke. She didn't worry. She just borrowed another violin and continued playing. Then the string broke again on the second violin! Everybody gasped. I'm sure most teenagers at this point would have broken down and cried...but not brave Midori. Once again she borrowed yet another violin. It was the first time she'd played on this violin and it was too big for her. But her playing was as good as

Everybody gasped when Midori's violin string broke.

ever. Everybody was surprised. When Midori finished the audience clapped for a very long time. Now when young Americans read her story they will feel very encouraged when things go wrong for them.

The next story is about rather a different kind of 'musician.' In fact it is a battery-operated toy flower. It is in the form of a rock musician. You may be surprised when you see it in action and it is called 'Flower Rock.' When 'Flower Rock' hears music or a voice it starts moving around and shaking just like Elvis Presley! They say that many young Japanese girls who love cute or 'kawaii' things are buying it. Some western people think that Japanese have difficulty

Which man will have the longest life?

in making new products. They can only copy. I don't think so. 'Flower Rock' is the first and only product of its kind in the world.

Indeed, some elderly western people get quite angry when they hear loud rock music. They shouldn't get angry because it's dangerous. Doctors now say that shouting and showing anger is very unhealthy. It's bad for the heart and makes your blood pressure go up. Doctors also used to think that 'workaholic' habits of busy people who do things too quickly, were also very bad for the heart. Now they say this is not true. Most busy people with too much to do are quite healthy. So maybe that is why Japanese now have the longest lives in the world. Although many Japanese are indeed 'workaholics,' they don't show so much anger. Also, it's healthier to eat sushi than beefsteaks!

Land in Tokyo now is so expensive and difficult to find. In fact more and more people are coming into Tokyo from the countryside. Soon, there will be more people in Tokyo than in the whole of Australia. So what can we do? One clever businessman is building a floating city in a kind of 'boat' in Tokyo Bay. Another idea is to build a whole city underground! Already a big construction company has a plan which you can see in the cartoon. They call it Alice City. You may remember 'Alice in Wonderland.' Alice found a whole new world underground after going down a rabbit hole. Of course, Alice City will be much better than a rabbit hole! Perhaps 100,000 people will live there. There

will be shops, offices, condominiums and maybe even a golf course! Sunlight will come in through a large glass dome at the top. Now it's only an idea but it's a very good one. In

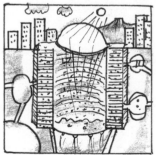

A future underground city in Japan called Alice City.

fact Japanese have more and better new ideas than anyone else these days.

Four Interesting People from Japan

When I first came to Japan, I used to write for various different newspapers including the Asahi Evening News. During this time I was lucky enough to interview many interesting Japanese people. This month I'd like to tell you something about them.

One of the most impressive people I met was a sumo wrestler called Taiho. Nowadays, he has lost a lot of weight but he was very big when I met him. Once, he said, he had been officially invited to France. I asked him whether he enjoyed the delicious French cuisine or cooking. He replied, "Not really because French people always talk too much when they're eating. I like to eat my food quickly and in silence like a samurai. That's the Japanese way and I think it's the best."

Of course Yukio Mishima was able to express his ideas very well, even in English which he spoke quite fast. He told me he

Yukio Mishima takes dictation from characters in his head.

never had any difficulty in finding ideas for his stories. His problem was that he couldn't write them down fast enough. That's why English translations of his books took four times as long as his original writing. He said, "The characters or people in my books live their own lives in my head. I never know what they are going to do or say. They always surprise me. Actually I just write everything down at their dictation. That's why I never have to work out a plot for my books in advance." Perhaps in the end, Mishima's thoughts were so strong he could not tell what was real and what was unreal. Perhaps his surprising act of *seppuku* was just part of his unreal world.

Then there was lively Yoshiko Ishii who more or less introduced French 'chanson' singing into Japan many years ago. She said she actually had no plan to stay in

France. Quite by chance, she found herself in Paris so she thought she would stay for a few days. While there she met a Monsieur Pasdoc. He offered her a singing contract to

'La Mysterieuse Orientale'

perform in his small theatre. So a few days became a few years. I asked her whether she spoke any French when she first arrived. "Not a word," she replied. "But that didn't worry me. Frenchmen like to do all the talking anyway. When I used to sit there in silence as if in deep Buddhist meditation, they quite admired me. They called me 'La Mysterieuse Orientale' (The Mysterious Oriental Lady). It was just because I could not understand them. When I started talking French quite fluently, they didn't like it so much. Perhaps I was no longer 'mysterious' to them!"

Another interesting Japanese singer I met went by the name of Akasaka Koume. She

Miss Koume (left) was a quick learner.

told me she had this name because before the war she had been the most famous geisha in Akasaka. She said at that time, girls from mining families were forced to be geisha. Their parents would receive a lump sum of money for their daughter's services. It was a kind of slavery. Her case was different. She came from a middle class professional family. As she wanted to be a geisha so badly, she had to run away from home. Her father was so angry that he refused to ever see or speak to her again. She said geisha training in those days was very hard and severe. Some girls would cry for hours because they couldn't get their body movements exactly right when opening and closing a door. She never had that problem because she was a quick learner. Asked about modern geisha, she said, "Really, they're just like office ladies or other salaried workers. When it's time for work, they just get into a sports car and drive to a *ryotei*. Once there, they put on a wig and kimono and act being geisha. We were REAL geisha 24 hours a day!" Later Miss Koume took up Japanese folk singing for which she became famous. During the war, a person was only allowed to have one job. So she had to give up being a geisha and be a full-time Japanese folk singer.

It was strange that both Miss Ishii and Miss Koume ended their interviews with almost the same words. "It's not enough for a top class singer to have a good voice, beauty and technique. They must have feeling, soul and a love for their fellow human beings." Perhaps that's the secret of their success and of all the other interesting Japanese people I met while I was a newspaperman.

What Is Japan's Biggest Problem in the Future?

Maybe Japan's biggest future problem, is, that nobody wants to work in factories. When students were questioned about their future jobs, most replied, "I'd like to work in the foreign section of a bank," "I'd like to work in the kabutocho somewhere" and so many wanted to work for trading companies. But very very few wanted to work in factories or manufacturing companies situated in the countryside. They could imagine themselves working out foreign currency

A future problem

'big deals' with a computer in a smart Marunouchi office. But they couldn't imagine themselves making parts for vacuum cleaners in Yamagata! It's a pity because

Japan's past and present strength has been its success in manufacturing. In a sense we can say blue collar jobs in factories are more important than white collar jobs in offices. They are basically important because they make things people need. Without factories, banks, computers, the stock exchange and trading companies could not exist. Factories can exist on their own. Of course there are thousands of young people in Thailand, the Philippines, Pakistan and other Asian countries who would do anything to work in Japanese factories. If Japanese don't want these jobs I think it's really a good idea to invite foreign workers to come to Japan. In fact if they don't have foreign labour, many small factories will go out of business. It will be Japan's biggest problem in the future.

Another problem is white collar crime. If you look at my cartoon, you may think Mr. B is the criminal. He is not. Mr. A is the criminal because he has stolen $6 million from a bank. He didn't steal the money with a gun but with a computer which is so much easier. Both in the States and in Japan white collar crime involving computers is rapidly

Which is the criminal?

A B

Can you guess?

increasing. They even have to have specially trained detectives. After all, it's much easier to press a computer button than to point a gun at someone.

Anyway, the interestingly named Ms. Kiss of West Germany has solved her problem. She found it very difficult to get a date because she was so fat. She found that many other fat people had the same problem so she started a 'fat people only' dating bureau. It is very successful. In fact many thin and slender people have rung her up because they prefer fat people too. Maybe if Mr. Powle's diet doesn't work he may get in touch with Ms. Kiss! In fact, 200 years ago 'fat' was fashionable in Europe. You only have to look at the paintings of the Dutch artist Rubens to understand that. It was only in the reign of Queen Victoria that small waists were thought to be beautiful as they are today.

One mother in Southampton, England solved her problem in a very unusual way. Her son had been knocked to the ground in a boxing match. When the referee had count-

The scene of a mother's love

ed to 8 her son was still on the ground. So his angry mother stepped into the boxing ring, took off one high-heeled shoe and started beating her son's opponent with it! Her son's opponent shouted, "No, don't do that. I surrender. I surrender." And so her son won the match but he was not very happy. Said he, "I want to fight the same man again. But next time it will be without my mother!"

Japan and My Family

In 1878 a young British doctor arrived in Yokohama. He was excited and loved everything he saw. Being very modern, he had a new invention. It was a camera. He took photographs of all that he saw: merchants, markets, sumo wrestlers, temples and even geisha girls. He wished that he could stay for a long time. Unfortunately he couldn't because he was the ship's doctor. But he really enjoyed his ten days in Emperor Meiji's Japan. Often he traveled by jinricksha. It's interesting to note that the jinricksha was not invented by a Chinese or a Japanese. It was actually invented by an American missionary in Japan! His wife

My grandfather in a jinricksha.

was very sick and he didn't have enough money to hire porters to carry her. So he invented the jinricksha so he could carry her himself. Later there were millions

My, father and his guide near Mount Fuji.

of jinrickshas all over Japan and China but the missionary remained poor because he couldn't patent his invention.

Anyway, I've got away from my story of the British doctor. I know all about him because he was my own grandfather. I really enjoyed looking at his photos of Japan in the Meiji Era. He also brought back many little ivory figures called *netsuke* and some beautiful woodblock prints. They must all be very valuable but unfortunately I don't know where they are now.

However there was one photo he didn't show us. We only found it among his things after he died. It was a photo of a beautiful Japanese girl in a kimono, probably in her early twenties. We laughed and said she must have been his first girl friend. Why would he keep the photo so secretly for such a long time? My grandmother didn't laugh. She said, "He never had any girl friends. I was his first and last love!" Since my grandmother was a very strong lady, nobody disagreed with her.

Later my father came to Japan too. That was aroud 1925. At that time he was working for the Hongkong and Shanghai Bank in Shanghai, China. In the summer it was so hot there that he came to Japan. He liked to stay in the Fujiya Hotel which is situated in Miyanoshita, Hakone. In fact, it was from there he wrote a letter to my mother asking for her hand in marriage. She said she would have to think about it. He asked her again when he went back to England. Luckily she agreed or you wouldn't be reading this story! My father remembers his guide. She told him when they were near Mount Fuji, "There's Mount Fuji. It means that either you or a member of your family will come back to Japan again."

Her words came true because here I am,

the third generation of Powles to come to Japan. But this is not my first visit. When I was 18, like all the other British boys, I had to join the army. One day I received a notice that I had to fight with the British army in Korea. I didn't even know where Korea was! I really did not understand why I had to risk my life fighting there. However, I was very lucky. Instead of going to Korea, I stayed in Kure near Hiroshima. I worked in the army records section. Like my father and grandfather before me, my happiest days have been spent in Japan. Of course the Japanese at that time were so poor. When I see the richly dressed people in Tokyo now, they are so different from the people I remember-

ed. However, although Japanese at that time were poor, they were not miserable. Even then I could admire their strong and cheerful spirit but I could never dream that Japan would

Japanese people now and as they used to be.

become so rich. Once, when I was going to Tokyo from Iwakuni in an American plane, I had a wonderful view of Mount Fuji. Like my father's guide, the pilot said, "That means you'll be coming back to Japan again."

Actually, I nearly didn't make it back again to Japan. My ship, named the Windrush, had trouble in the Mediterranean. For some reason, the engine exploded. Soon we had to jump off the ship because it was sinking. Luckily, the weather was good and the sea was calm so most of us lived to tell the story. And I lived to come back to Japan just as the American pilot had predicted.

Japanese Bosses and American Workers

As the Japanese yen gets higher and higher, more Japanese businessmen are buying land and companies in America. They are so cheap compared with those in Japan. For instance a Japanese motor tire company bought a factory of an American tire company. It was losing a lot of money each year. Originally, there were a thousand workers. Now there were only six hundred. Four hundred had lost their jobs. That was four years ago. What happened when a Japanese company bought the old tire factory? You can find out by reading this story. It is written in the imaginary words of Bob Roberts. He's not a real person but he could

Japanese are buying many American buildings and companies.

be. Well, let's hear what Bob Roberts has to say.

Yes, my tire company was in a very bad way. I was very worried because I was going to lose my job. We only produced 700 tires a day and we were losing money. Then we heard that the factory had been bought by a big Japanese company. Actually, we were not very happy when we first heard the news. We thought we'd have to work with very few holidays. I think that's what Japanese do. When the Japanese businessmen arrived, they had a meeting with our labour union men. It went very badly with a lot of angry words. Finally our union boss shouted, "We must work OUR way. Please get out of the room right now!" Not only did the Japanese businessmen leave the room, but they flew all the way back to Tokyo!

We were very angry with our union boss. We wanted to keep our jobs and we knew that Japanese business methods had worked very well in other American companies. At last the union leader wrote to Tokyo to say he was very sorry he had lost his temper. He apologized and hoped the Japanese would come back again. This time he promised to be friendly.

Before the Japanese take-over.

When the Japanese business-men came back they were very polite. They didn't talk about that bad meeting. Of course there were many changes in the factory but they were changes for the better. For a start all the four hundred workers who had lost their jobs were given their old jobs back again. This created a very good feeling. Even our union leader, who had been very rude, agreed that the Japanese managers were the best.

Also we didn't have to work as hard as we thought. At great cost the best and newest machinery was put into our factory. As a worker I can tell you it's much better to operate new machinery. It's more enjoyable, safer and makes you feel better. Also you can produce more without working harder.

After the Japanese take-
over

Under the old system we only used to make 700 tires a day. Now we make 3,000! In a way, I suppose we do work harder. We have a lot of overtime. But when we are paid an extra $20 an hour overtime, we are happy. I know my wife is. We have moved into a bigger house and my two children will soon be going to college. In the old days I would never have been able to think of such a thing. My wife also says she even enjoys shopping more. Why? Because the Japanese have imported a lot of cherry trees from Tokyo. They have planted these cherry trees along the shopping mall and in the park. We even have our own cherry blossom drinking parties and picnics! I think that is a very nice Japanese custom indeed.

Another thing that we American workers like, is, that our ideas seem important to the Japanese. Our American bosses never used to ask us about our ideas. "You are paid to work, not to think" was their attitude. Now we often have meetings with our Japanese managers. We can make suggestions and have ideas on how to make the business better. The Japanese always happily agree with us ... even if they sometimes do nothing about it. Often they do. For example they were going to build another tire factory costing $70 million. It would have been built in another town far away. We didn't like this because we wanted our friends and relatives to have good jobs in the new factory too. We wanted it in our town. At first, the Japanese managers didn't like our idea as they had already made their plans. Finally, to our great happiness, the head office in Tokyo agreed to build the new factory right beside the old one. The American company would never have listened to our ideas in the first place. They certainly would never changed their plans to please us.

Actually, the Japanese don't meet us much after work. I have one friend Hiroshi Saito. He said it was the same with American business executives in Tokyo who spend most of their time in the American Club. Anyway, Japanese tend to just have social meetings together. Hiroshi says they actually want to be friendly. But most of them don't speak English very well. Well, I expect that too will change in time. All I can say, is, that Japanese are very welcome in the United States as far as I'm concerned.

This fictional account is based on a true case with very few changes. Maybe YOU might be a Japanese manager posted to America one day. Please study English hard then you can have a much more enjoyable time.

The British Art of Lifemanship

A lot of people sometimes say it's difficult to meet British people. It seems they try to be so superior in everything. If you talk about music, writing or climbing up mountains it appears that British people always know more than you do. Of course, I'm British myself but this is what I have heard from people who come from other countries.

Actually, the key word to the problem is to "appear" to know more than anyone else. In fact, many British don't know more. We call the art of appearing to be superior without being so "One-Upmanship" or Lifemanship. You're one-up when you are able to make somebody else feel uncomfortable or inferior through your superior knowledge, wit or general background. We call such an unpleasant person "a Lifeman".

For example, you might be talking about the finer points of Beethoven's 9th Symphony. The British lifeman will be looking

Of course you know Johannes Givensius.

A lifeman in action

at you very closely without blinking his eyes. Already you are beginning to feel uncomfortable. Then he may say, "I like Johannes Givensius, the little known composer of the early 15th Century. Of course you know that Beethoven copied a lot of his choral work for his compositions." Of course you don't know this. And the British lifeman knows you don't know ... so he's one-up already. The fact that no such person as Johannes Givensius ever existed is not really important. British lifeman has already established his superiority.

There are lifeladies as well. Let us say that a Noriko Suzuki has studied lifemanship. She meets a rather unpleasantly superior English lady. Noriko may say to her, "I like those pearls you are wearing. They look almost real. But I know they're not real. They're false. Naturally I am wearing

REAL pearls. You can see the difference, can't you?"

A lifelady in action

Will the superior English lady feel ashamed of her false pearls? Not at all. She will say, "Yes, I USED to have a necklace just the same as yours." After making sure Noriko is wearing cultured pearls, she will continue, "Have you thought of all the SUFFERING that your necklace has caused? Do you know that a little bead is put into the shell of a poor oyster? The oyster's whole life is a painful torture which never stops. The pain hurts the oyster so much that he coats it with pearl or shall we say his tears. After that his shell is pulled apart and he dies! No, I'm happy with my false pearls and you can be happy with your REAL ones."

After this you might think that Noriko will be quiet. Perhaps in shame she will go to the Ladies toilet, take off her necklace

Being 'one-up' and 'one-down' with a mink coat.

and leave quietly by the back door. But she doesn't because she's a fighter. She's not going to be defeated in the One-Upmanship contest. What's more, she's spent four years at the London School of Economics so she knows what it's all about.

She says very sweetly, "Perhaps you are ignorant about marine life in the sea. In fact oysters are cold-blooded. Marine scientists say they can't feel anything. By the way, how many adorable, lovable cute warm-blooded little animals in the prime of their little lives were killed to make your mink coat?"

The English lady is usually NEVER at a loss for words. However she is now silent and everybody looks at her in an amused way. If Noriko wants to be really cruel, she may add, "You don't know. I guess about 40 little minks were murdered just to provide one coat for YOU. Of course I could NEVER wear a coat like that. But you can. You look so beautiful in it. I must go now. But please enjoy the party." Noriko now leaves with a superior little smile knowing that she's now one-up. She knows the English lady will NOT enjoy the party now.

Well there you have a few basic facts about lifemanship. Naturally this essay is not meant to be serious. If you are lucky enough to have a pearl necklace or a mink coat, don't worry too much. Also if you meet English person who APPEARS to be very superior, you don't have to worry too much either!

When Is a British Public School Not a Public School?

In England when we talk about public schools, they are not public. In fact they are very expensive private schools. Then why are they called public schools when they are really private? It's because they once were public and nobody has bothered to change their description. For example my own school, Tonbridge, was founded in 1548 for the sons of poor people who couldn't afford private teachers. It's amazing to think Tonbridge first received its charter from the boy King Edward VI over 400 years ago and boys have been receiving education there ever since!

Of course the type of student has gradually changed. The education received there was so good that the children of the wealthy wanted to be students too. Actually my father was not wealthy at all but he was prepared to make sacrifices so I should get a good education.

Still despite the high quality of education, many think public schools should be shut down because they promote class distinction. They wrongly think public schoolboys

Some people imagine public school boys are 'snobs' like this.

are unpleasant 'snobs'. A snob is someone who looks down upon or despises others because he thinks he is wealthier or superior. Later it is thought such public schoolboy snobs get the best places in the universities and the best jobs through the 'old boy' network. This is not true. In fact British universities are much more democratic than those in Japan or America. For instance entrance to an Oxford or a Cambridge college is almost always by scholarship. This means that most university education is paid for by the state so that a talented poor boy has a better chance of success than a rich boy of average intelligence.

One problem, is, that the class system may

Discipline was very strict.

be kept on by the way people speak. A boy or girl who has been educated in a government school in Liverpool may have a northern Liverpool accent like the Beatles. If a boy is educated at a government school in the London area then he may have a strong cockney accent. A public school boy will usually speak the Queen's English or BBC English, as it is termed. Happily, accents don't matter so much nowadays. Top positions in Britain are now decided by ability and qualifications, not by having the 'right' accent.

Are public schools comfortable with good facilities? No, they are not. Let me tell you something about them. I entered Tonbridge at the age of 13. I had to sleep on a very hard bed in a dormitory with 30 other boys. We had to get up at 6 a.m. and then take an ice-cold shower even in the middle of the coldest winter. Just once a week we were allowed to take a 30-minute bath. If we were 31 minutes taking a bath we got a 'black mark'. If we got six black marks then we were punished. At this time I was forced to put my head under the table while I was beaten hard with a stick. Yes, discipline was very strict. If we received six black marks we then received six black marks on our upper legs!

One could get black marks for anything. For reading a book with a flashlight after 9 p.m. 'lights out', putting your hands in your pockets, or going out with a girl friend. Once when I was caught by my house master with my girl friend, I was very ashamed because I told a lie. I said she was

'my sister'. The master then said, "That's interesting. May I ask your sister the address of her house?" When she was silent, it was obvious I was not being truthful. That earned me six

"My sister, Sir!"

black marks all at once!

Actually, the sports facilities were excellent. We had the choice of playing rugby, cricket, fives, squash and tennis. In the winter I chose rugby and tennis in the summer. Of course, British people generally follow cricket matches as eagerly as Japanese and Americans follow baseball but frankly I find both games rather boring. You may not agree but I think rugby and tennis are much more active and exciting.

Will Tonbridge and other British public schools continue for another 400 years? It's difficult to say. The Socialists want to shut them down because they say these schools are the root cause of class distinction. I don't think so. They give the best available education and have provided many of Britain's great leaders in the past. I hope they will continue to do so for many years to come.

Hardships
of the British Army

If you met me now, I don't think you could ever imagine that I was once a soldier. I'm not at all a military-type of person. But, yes, when I was 18, I joined the British army. I didn't do it because I wanted to. It was the law then that when a boy became 18, he had to become a soldier whether he liked it or not. I didn't like it. And my mother was upset too because she thought I might get killed in the war which was then taking place in Korea. Many British boys had been killed there.

I tried to comfort her by telling her that I was a man now and that this was a good chance to see the world. "And the next world too if you get killed in Korea," she replied. She then remembered I had flat feet. If you have flat feet you soon get tired when marching or standing around. She thought if the army doctor saw me with flat feet, I wouldn't have to join the army. After think-

ORRIBLE NIGNOGS!

My introduction into the British army.

ing awhile she said, "If you keep jumping off the kitchen table, you could make your feet flatter than ever!"

In spite of my mother's impractical suggestions, I reported to an army barracks to become a soldier. I shall never forget my first day. About 50 unhappy young men lined up on the parade ground. In front of us was a very cruel-looking man in uniform with a loud unpleasant voice. He shouted at us, "What a weak, ugly, dirty, poor lot you are! Even if I called you pigs, I think pigs would feel bad! Well, I'll get you nignogs into good shape... if it kills me. Do you know what a nignog is?" At this point in his 'charming' greeting he stopped in front of one poor man who confessed he didn't know what a nignog was. "It's a fat fairy in boots... and that's what you are!"

We were then marched very quickly, while

the sergeant shouted, "Left-right-left-right-left-right." It was a pity that every time he shouted "left" it was my right foot which went forward instead of the left. Of course, the

A Nignog

sergeant soon noticed. "Your feet seem as stupid as the look on your face. Run round the parade ground 8 times so that your stupid feet will obey my commands." Oh, how I hated the army!

Although I was nearly dead after all that running, I had to report to the clothing store. Inside, two badly fitting uniforms were thown at me and a most uncomfortable pair of boots. When I complained that I'd always had my shoes specially made to measure because I had flat feet which were 'difficult', I was told, "Well, you now have boots which are 'difficult'. That will be a change for you." We were then hurried to the cookhouse where we were given old tin

Which soldier is Mr. Powle?

plates. We then lined up again to get "beef stew" from the cook. Actually, it was just fat and potato without any taste. It was quite a long time before I got used to army food. I lost a lot of weight.

We were then marched "left-right-left-right" to the dormitories. We had to undress, wash and be in bed within five minutes. That was alright but it was the unpleasant smell I didn't like. I'm not a snob but I had to agree with the novelist George Orwell's interesting comment that you can tell the difference between lower and high class men in England by the smell of their socks. I don't think there were many high class men in that dormitory!

Anyway, in spite of the hard bed, grey blankets, and the absence of sheets, I slept quite well. In fact I dreamt I was back in my comfortable bedroom at home. However, it was like a bad dream when I woke up at 5 a.m. in the morning. It was still dark and the sergeant was banging his stick on the table to wake us up. I was reminded of some lines in a popular song which go, "This is the army Mr. Jones. No private rooms with telephones. You've had your breakfast in bed before. But you won't get it there anymore!" How true! After a breakfast which was worse than dinner, I found myself on the parade ground again . . . and was last again. And of course, my enemy the sergeant was waiting for me. He asked me why I was so slow. I replied, "Actually, I thought . . . ." At that point he interrupted me with, "In this army you do not think. You only obey. Now run around the parade ground 10 times." I hated the British army more than ever.

That's an account of my first and worst day. In the end I really had a very good time. Because of my military training at school I was finally made an officer. However, my mother almost died when I received orders to go to Korea. "Now, don't try and be brave, Brian," she said. "With your flat feet you belong in an office." She needn't have worried. I never reached Korea. I stopped and stayed in Japan. And I liked it so much that I've come back again!

Let's Meet England's Royals

Like Japan, England is very lucky to have a nice royal family. I think kings and queens are much more interesting and glamourous than presidents and First Ladies, don't you?

I know I was very excited to meet Queen Elizabeth personally when she came to Japan many years ago. It was in a park in Shinjuku. All the British community were lined up to see her. Then my heart almost stopped when she spoke to me. She asked me, "And what do you do?" I had my answer ready. "I teach the Queen's English, Your Majesty. That's the best English there is." She laughed and said she agreed. Well, that was my brief moment of glory. It

My brief moment of glory

would have been nice if she had invited me for tea in Buckingham Palace. So far I've had no invitation!

I suppose the Queen Mother is the most popular member of our Royal Family. Although she's getting on for ninety years old, she's still very active. She travels abroad and opens hospitals. She certainly must have been a very good mother. When Queen Elizabeth was only a Princess she attended her first cocktail party. Princess Elizabeth (as she was then) was very happy when somebody offered her a glass of wine. However, the Queen Mother was just behind her and said, "I don't think we're quite ready for wine yet, dear. Let's put the wine back and have a nice glass of healthy orange juice." No doubt the Queen was disappointed but she always obeyed her strong mother.

Of course, the Queen is very lucky in having nice children too. Prince Charles with his cheerful smile and big ears is also very popular. Recently he has been very angry with modern architects in London. He says the old city and especially the River Thames has been spoiled by big ugly skyscrapers. I and many British people agree with him but the architects don't.

There's no doubt that the most photographed member of the Royal Family is his

Prince Charles does NOT like modern architecture.

beautiful wife Princess Diana. Slender and fashionable, she seems to wear a different dress and hat every day. Some say she spends too much money on clothes. I don't think so. She helps the British fashion industry. Of course she has different tastes from Prince Charles as she is much younger. She likes disco music and dancing. John Travolta said she was an expert. Prince Charles prefers opera and classical music.

Another of the Queen's sons is Prince Andrew who is considered quite handsome by the ladies. He is very brave and flew in a helicopter during the war in the Falkland Islands. The Queen was quite worried when he invited a beautiful cabaret dancer to

Princess Diana (left) has a different style from Fergie (right).

Buckingham Palace! Now he's safely married to a nice girl called Fergie. Fergie sometimes wears strange but interesting clothes which they say the stylish Princess Diana docs not approve of. She also wrote a very popular children's book called 'Budgie.' 'Budgie' is the name of a helicopter which is almost human and has many adventures. There is only one problem about this book. As a member of the Royal Family, Fergie should give all the profits to charity to help people. However, she wants to keep most of the money herself. She has been criticized for this. But then she is only human too!

Princess Anne is the Queen's only daughter. She is so good at riding horses that she was a member of Britain's Olympic riding team. Her husband Mark Phillips loves horses as well. Their marriage seemed to be a fairy-tale romance. But now they are separated and no one knows whether she will get a divorce like her Aunt Princess Margaret. If she does, the British public will not worry because they say it is just part of modern life.

Actually, some time ago I was asking some of my younger Japanese students if they knew the name of the Queen of England. One little boy put up his hand, He said, "I know. It's Mrs Thatcher!" Yes, she may sometimes think of herself as a queen but even she can't be a member of the Royal Family!

Scuba Diving
in the Philippines

Have you ever dreamt of scuba diving under the ocean? Swimming under the water with an oxygen tank among corals and tropical fish really does seem like a dream. Well, at last my dream came true two months ago.

First of all, I found a dream of a tropical island. It is called Borocay Island in the Philippines and it just takes an hour by air from Manila. Indeed it was beautiful. Coconut palm trees seemed to dance in the wind over snowy white beaches. The sea was a turquoise blue. And if my hotel was a little rough, the price was right ... ¥750 a night! Of course this was the out-of-season rate. Then in the evening you can choose from a multitude of international restaurants: Swiss, French, German, Thai etc. Maybe the dinner prices are half of what you would pay in Manila but a fifth of what you would pay in Tokyo! Then there is a disco where you can dance away until the early morning hours in the open air under the stars. Then the cocktails ... well, I must get on to the subject of my scuba diving. My friends tell me when I get onto the subject of food and drink, I get carried away and can go on forever!

I was introduced by my hotel owner to an excellent Filipino scuba diving instructor called Boyet. Somehow I imagined myself immediately putting on an oxygen tank, diving into the sea and then have tropical fish eating food out of my hand. You know, like you see on the television programmes. No, it wasn't like that. To get your scuba diving license, you have to memorize the contents of a 200-page book and then be tested on it. It was like being at school again. Boyet said, "It's very important because your life may depend on it." Indeed he was right. Four days later, a German did not listen to the advice of his Filipino diving companion. During his first dive he had seen a most wonderful coral reef. He said he would go deeper on his second dive. His companion said, "It's very dangerous to go

My stomach just wouldn't fit into the wet suit.

deeper during your second dive." He went anyway. But he was never seen again although helicopters looked for him for many hours. Perhaps he was carried out to the open sea by a strong current and then eaten by sharks.

Finally, I was ready for my first dive. Boyet gave me a black rubber wet suit to wear. Of course, I was quite fat after eating all that gourmet food. No matter how much I pushed, pulled and squeezed, I just could not fit into that wet suit. One person said, "It's like Cinderella's ugly sister trying to put the glass slipper on." I was very ashamed to hear such an unkind remark! Some laughing children nearby made me feel more ashamed.

After giving up on the wet suit, I went out to sea in Boyet's boat. I was fitted out with an oxygen tank, respirator, BVD jacket and other equipment. I could hardly move because it was all so unfamiliar and heavy. Then Boyet said, "When I count to three, roll backwards into the sea." He counted, "One, two, three" But I didn't move. The truth, is, that I was afraid to. I think I would rather have jumped off the top of the tall Sumitomo Building in Shinjuku. For the second time, I felt very ashamed. The count started again. "One, two, three . . . ." This time it was different. Although it felt like committing hara-kiri, I took a deep breath, shut my eyes and rolled overboard. Well, I'm still alive to tell the story. Boyet followed me diving under the surface of the water. I tried to follow him but I couldn't. I just stayed on the surface. And yet I was pumping all the oxygen out of my jacket as hard as I could. Finally I sank to the bottom of the ocean like a stone. When I hit the bottom there was a cloud of sand and all the fish swam away as

I went DOWN like a stone and UP like a bottle cork.

A 30-dollar-view under the ocean is better than a 12-million-view in space.

quickly as possible. I don't blame them. Maybe they thought I was some kind of bomb! I saw Boyet floating above me. I was flat on my back. Once again I couldn't move. So this time I pumped a lot of oxygen IN to the jacket. Then I shot up to the surface of the sea like a bottle cork! I was going up and down like a child's yoyo! Of course the secret is in breathing and controlling the oxygen flow.

Once you have mastered that, scuba diving is a wonderful experience. You can see live shells walking about on the ocean floor. Corals of every shape, size and dimension, like fairy castles, surround you. You enter the silent secret world of exotic colourful tropical fish, crabs and lobsters. And just the fact of swimming, breathing, seeing and moving in a fantastic underwater world, is like a fantasy.

I have heard that $12 million was spent to put a Japanese journalist called Akiyama into a Soviet space rocket. What did he see? Almost nothing except for clouds and blue sky. And yet for $30 or less you can hire all the equipment and a boat to explore a fantastic world under the ocean. That is much better value I think!

Exotic Adventure Holidays

Maybe you have just returned from your New Year's holiday. Some of you may have been to Hawaii, Hongkong or even Europe. But next time why not try something different? There are now one or two travel agencies specializing in 'adventure tours'. For example, you could go to see an Antarctic ice pack. Penguins may greet you with their love dance against the dramatic background of huge walls of ice. If you want something warmer, why not try exploring among the wild Asmat tribes in New Guinea? You'll see Asmat natives, their bodies covered in war paint, will stage a special fight for you. Or you could see the wild life in

See a penguin love dance in the Antarctic.

Africa on a 'tent safari'. It's very exciting to shoot lions and elephants close up . . . but only with your camera of course. One 82-year old grandmother said her one wish was to

Enjoy a cup pf coffee on a 'tent Safari'!

photograph the giant 4-metre-lizards on Komodo Island in Indonesia. She was quite sick while doing the seven-kilometre-trek. But she kept saying, "I want to see those Komodo dragons once before I die." And she did. If you want, you can go in a canoe up part of the giant Amazon river. But don't put your hand in the water or it may become 'piranha bento'! If you're the energetic kind, you can go mountaineering in Nepal. Of course, if you go on these adventure tours, you will have to put up with a lot of hardships. There will be extremes of hot and cold temperatures. You may have to carry your own baggage a lot of the way. There could be poisonous snakes and mosquitoes.

Put up with hardship

For example, a Lindblad Travel ship had to be quickly abandoned on its way to the Antarctic. It was in danger of sinking. Luckily, everyone was rescued by a ship of the Chilean navy. Surprisingly, most of the passengers returned the next year to take the same trip again! Said one passenger, "It was the excitement and danger which made it the trip of a lifetime. I'm tired of staying at 5-star hotels in cities around the world." Also, such trips are not cheap in spite of rough conditions. For example, a month-long cruise down the Yangtse River to Shanghai may cost around $10,000. But it's a trip you'll never forget!

Frankly, I haven't been on any of these exotic trips myself. Perhaps, I'm not adventurous or rich enough. However, I have had my share of interesting travels. Let me tell you about going to London via Moscow.

First you take a ship from Yokohama to the port of Nahodka. Then you go by train to Khabarovsk through Siberia. From there you take an Ilyushin jet to Moscow. After a few days there, you can take a train to Helsinki via Leningrad. Then by boat and train to London. That journey is quite an adventure too.

Adventures in the USSR

One of the most interesting ways to get to London, is through the Soviet Union. Of course, this country has its problems so you may have problems too. However, I prefer to think of them not as problems but as adventures. And I love adventures. Anyway, let me tell you about my travel adventures in that country.

First, you go by a Soviet passenger ship from Yokohama to Nahodka. It's an exciting moment as the ship leaves its dock at Yokohama. People are laughing, crying and very emotional. Finally, the ship moves and one by one, all the colourful paper streamers break. Of course, one end of the streamer is held by a passenger on the ship and the other end by the loved one on land. Gradually Japan disappears into the distance. You are out in the open sea. This is REAL travel. It's so different from going by air.

Then you make your way to your cabin. I

had some interest-
ing people in mine.
For example there
was an Austrian
man. He said he
was teaching
Crown Princess
Michiko (as she
was then) to play
the harp. Then

The emotion of REAL travel

there were two boys, both nineteen years old
who were going to tour Europe for two
years by bicycle. They were going to start
from Helsinki and go by slow stages to
Rome. They would get money by working
at odd jobs on the way. They were REAL
travellers. So different from young people
going on packaged tours!

Soon the dinner bell was ringing. As
expected, we started off with delicious
borscht soup made from cabbage. Unfortunately the steak that followed was not so
good. It looked like, tasted like and felt like
shoe leather! It was so tough I had to leave
it on my plate. The motherly-looking waitress, however, was quite angry with me for

The waitress was motherly but severe.

not eating the tough meat. Very severely she told me in broken English, "Many hungry are. Ees good meat. You eat meat. Eat delicious meat." I was very surprised to be addressed in such a way by a waitress. Then I reminded myself I was going to the peoples' paradise where everybody was equal; obediently I ate my meat.

After two days or so, we arrived at the port of Nahodka. Here we immediately boarded an old fashioned but comfortable train which reminded me of the one I'd seen in the movie "The Oriental Express". It was very pleasant travelling through Siberia while drinking Russian style tea with strawberry jam in it. Next morning we arrived at Khabarovsk which is the capital city of Siberia. My first impression of this city was that everything was very big compared with Japan . . . big streets, big squares, big monu-

ments and big ladies!   They are big because
they eat a lot of bread, potatoes, and fatty
meat. Ice cream is also delicious and popular
but I had to wait for over an hour before I
was served at an ice cream stand.

We also had to wait for a long time for our
plane to take off from Khabarovsk airport
to fly to Moscow. When I asked an Intourist
official about the time of departure, she
replied brusquely, "When there are enough
people to fill the plane. It might be in one
hour but it might be one day."

In fact, it was one day. At last we entered
the giant Illyushin jet. It made so much
noise and shook so much before taking off,
that it made me think I was in the stomach
of a giant dinosaur. It was not so comfortable because it had to be changed into a
military fighter plane at a moment's notice.
However, I was able to chat with the beautiful blonde stewardess. Her English was
excellent. She told me that she was a student
of Moscow university and her job on the
plane was only a kind of 'arbeit'. Anyway,
we were served delicious snacks which in-
cluded a pot of REAL caviare. The two

Japanese students next to me didn't seem to like their caviare as they didn't touch it. So I'm ashamed to say I asked if I could eat theirs. After some time, they asked, "By the way what WAS that strange black stuff?" On being informed that it was real expensive caviare they looked very surprised. "Oh, we didn't know. We'd like to eat caviare once in our lives." "I'm sorry," I replied, "It's already been eaten!" It was true but I felt very greedy.

After a long journey, we finally arrived at Moscow airport. Of course everybody's baggage had arrived . . . except mine! I was not very pleased to learn that it had been left behind in Siberia! Then a very large imposing lady told us she was going to read our names from a list. When we heard our names called, we were to say, "Present". She would then tell us the name of the hotel where we were to stay. She was like a strict school mistress. Of course, every name was called . . . except mine! When I asked her about my hotel she replied, "I don't know. You are NOT on my list." The fact that I was not on her list seemed to indicate that I didn't exist.

Anyway, they booked me into the Metropole, the oldest hotel in Moscow, built before the revolution. In Tokyo I'd paid for a reserved first-class single room

I dreamed I was like James Bond.

with bath. Actually, I got a third class room which I had to share with another and no bathroom. When I complained about this to the Intourist office, I was told, "You are lucky to get any room at all at this busy time of year."

I must say the Intourist guides are excellent. My reception in Leningrad was quite different from that in Moscow. No sooner had the train stopped in the station, than a very pretty girl entered the carriage. I was amazed when she came straight up to me and said, "Welcome to Leningrad Mr. Powle." To this day, I don't know how she recognized me or knew where I would be at that moment. But perhaps the KGB did!

This was ten years ago and at that time they knew everything about everybody.

In fact, the London travel agent warned me on my return journey to be very careful about what I said in my hotel room. He said, "It may be bugged with listening devices hidden in the ceiling or in the lamp. Also, you may be approached by beautiful KGB spies to worm out your secrets." He made me feel like James Bond. On my way back, I tried to look clever and secretive but no beautiful KGB spy approached me. What a pity!

I hope this account of my travel and troubles, won't put you off going to Russia. I understand the service is much better nowadays. It's much more interesting than going to Europe directly by air. And travelling by ship, train and plane gives you a sense of REAL travel. You should try it!

Strange and Funny Happenings

A lot of us feel tired at this time of year. Perhaps you have a cold which makes you feel ill and unhappy. Apart from taking medicine what can we do about our winter problems? How can we make ourselves feel happy?

Doctors say laughter is the best medicine. So ... if you can think of something funny which makes you laugh, you'll feel better and happier. So here are some strange and funny happenings. I hope they may make you laugh and feel better.

Who is this famous man?

The first incident happened in the land surrounding ex-President Reagan's California house. Some security guards saw a strange man with a strange face. They arrested him and shouted at him. They asked him if he had a bad purpose in coming to Mr. Reagan's house. The strange man replied, "I am President Reagan!" Then they said they didn't know him because his face was so strange. His face was strange because he had put anti-wrinkle cream on his face. He had special cream to smooth out the many lines on his face. Of course, he wanted to look nice and young for his Tokyo visit . . . when he was getting $2 million for it!

Can watching sumo be dangerous? A 74-year-old man found out that it could be very dangerous. He was a real sumo fan and he was very happy to get a front row seat.

Suddenly and without any warning . . .

Suddenly, and without any warning, the two huge sumo wrestlers fell right on top of him! At first some people wondered if he had been killed. He was taken to hospital.

Luckily, his injuries were not serious. He was soon able to leave the hospital. He was lucky one of the wrestlers was not Konishiki or he might have had to stay in hospital longer. Perhaps he won't sit in the front row any more and I don't think I will either!

Although we know that railway men do useful jobs we never think about them much. But perhaps they are very interesting. There's no doubt that five railwaymen working in JR's Hakata station are interesting. They were guests at a JR-sponsored party at a Saga hotel. Perhaps the party was a bit quiet. They thought they would do something to 'spice it up' and make it lively. They took off all their clothes and did a nude dance! They did it because they thought the customers, both men and women, would be pleased by their dance. However, the station master of Hakata was NOT pleased. In fact he was very angry. He took the five JR 'dancers' into another room and punched them. Perhaps he shouldn't have done it because he had to resign from his job. I think clipping tickets and pushing people into trains must be difficult some-

My student's strangest experience

times. It's only natural they should want to relax and have fun. However, if you're invited to a JR party you can't expect nude dancing every time!

The next incident isn't funny but it's interesting. Last week I asked my students to tell me about their strangest experience. One girl told me when she was in South Africa, she had ridden an ostrich like a horse. It was most uncomfortable so she wanted to get off. But she couldn't because the ostrich would not stop. She shouted, "Help me. Help me." But nobody could as the ostrich ran around faster and faster. At last it stopped so she was alright. So I think if anybody asks you to ride an ostrich, it's best to say, "No thank you." By the way, did you know that an ostrich egg is the biggest in the world and you can make seven omelettes out of one egg! Perhaps my student's ostrich was angry at having her eggs made into omelettes.

Michael Jackson's Difficult Situation

A jeweller in Los Angeles was very worried recently. A very strange and suspicious-looking man entered his jewellery shop. The strange man wanted to look at only the most expensive diamond rings. The jeweller wondered how such a man could afford such high-priced rings. He thought that the man might be a jewel thief. So he called the police. Ten minutes later three police cars surrounded his shop. A policeman went up to the strange-looking man and asked him who he was. "I'm Michael Jackson." was the surprising reply. This made the policeman angry. He said, "If you're Michael Jackson then I'm President

Are you ... Michael Jackson?

Bush." Then the strange-looking man took off a wig and other false hair. He REALLY was Michael Jackson!" Michael Jackson explained, "When I go shopping I have to go in

This is you in 20 year's time.

disguise with a wig and other accessories. If my fans recognized me, they would mob me and I couldn't escape." The jeweller and the policeman were at a loss for words in this situation.

Scott Barrows of the University of Illinois can tell you how your face will look in 20 year's time. He does this with the aid of a computer. Of course I think most ladies wouldn't want to know! However, such knowledge can sometimes be useful. For instance Janet Hicks was worried about her two daughters. Her husband had left her and taken her two daughters with him. For 12 years she could hardly get a minute's sleep. She was worrying about them all the time. She searched and searched but she couldn't find them. Then she heard about Scott Barrows. She gave him some old photos of her daughters. In a short time he soon produced computer-made pictures of how they would look at the present time. The pictures were shown on television. Within ten minutes there were calls on the special hot line. A lady said the girls were living in a house next to hers. The very next morning the happy mother was reunited with her two daughters and her husband was under arrest. Of course, Janet thanked Scott Barrows for his help but her husband did not! One newspaper has asked Barrows to reconstruct President Kennedy and Marilyn Monroe as they would look now as senior citizens in their seventies. But I don't think this is a good idea. I'd prefer to remember them as they were. Anyway, perhaps quite a few of the thousands of missing children who are lost in the U.S. can be found with the aid of computers. Wives can find missing husbands too. But maybe they don't want to be found!

Japanese have so many difficulties in

speaking English.
Probably pronun-
ciation is the most
difficult problem.
For instance, I was
surprised when a
Japanese guest
asked me if she
could take a bath
at my house late at

I wanted GLOVES not a GLOBE!

night. Actually she meant "take a BUS." In a way I was a little disappointed! Another time a 70-year-old man asked his American friend if he could get some GLOVES for him. He was very surprised to receive a GLOBE! Although westerners are sure that the pronunciation of GLOVES and GLOBE are quite different, Japanese may pronounce them in the same way. In another case a Japanese customer asked to start his dinner with soup at an American restaurant. He was very surprised too when the waiter replied, "You can find it in the toilet!" The waiter thought the Japanese man had said SOAP not SOUP. Recently at Aoyama Gakuin I asked a student after I had been talking for a while, "Do you underSTAND?" To everybody's amusement and my surprise, he suddenly stood up. He only understood the 'stand' part of 'underSTAND'. Perhaps Japanese shouldn't pronounce things very well. Otherwise we wouldn't get so many humorous situations!

Unhappiness Made These People Famous!

Do you feel unhappy sometimes? Maybe, you're not doing so well at school. Perhaps you've been punished or you have to do something you don't like. If so, don't worry. You must just go on until you succeed. We say, "If at first you don't succeed, try, try and try again." If you do this, your unhappiness will actually make you stronger. You must be happy to have problems! This month I will tell you about five people who had problems and it was these problems which made them world famous.

In the first picture you see a young man being arrested a long time ago. He has just shot a deer with his bow and arrow. He is very

William Shakespeare

unhappy because the deer belonged to a rich lord and he could be punished by being put to death! He has a wife who is eight years older than he is. They have two children. Luckily, he escaped. But he travelled around doing many different jobs. He also fell in love with a dark-eyed lady. But according to his sad poetry, she did not love him! This story is probably true but we are not sure as it happened so long ago. The young man was the famous poet and dramatist, William Shakespeare!

This young man is being shouted at by his angry father. He has failed his examination. "You will never do well. I am ashamed of you." shouts the father. After this, the little

Winston Churchill

boy tried to do everything better than anybody else. Even after his father died, he kept his fighting spirit. He was determined that he would be good so his father would never have to be ashamed of him. He grew up to be Sir Winston Churchill, the great British wartime leader and the most famous Englishman of this century!

Adolf Hitler

This poor artist is trying to sell his pictures of churches in Vienna. Nobody wants to buy them, so he has to go without his dinner. Twice he has tried to enter the Vienna art school and twice he has failed. Later he ruled almost the whole of Europe and millions of people died because of him. He is Adolf Hitler. If he could have entered the art school, he might just have been a poor but happy artist. History would also have been different and many others would have been much happier too! In this case, it's a pity that this evil man did succeed, although he was defeated in the end because he was such a bad man.

Here we see a strange man with an orange-coloured beard. He is an artist and

Vincent Van Gogh

he just can't stop painting. He is in the lunatic asylum because people think he is mad. Right now you see him painting some sunflowers. But nobody wants to buy his paintings because they seem to be so strange. In his whole lifetime he only sold one painting for a small sum of money. Somebody was sorry for him. Of course, he's dead now. But can you believe that a Japanese company paid around $25 million for that painting of sunflowers? Naturally, because the mad artist was Vincent Van Gogh.

This girl is a member of a very rich British family. She's travelled around Europe. She goes to dances and champagne parties every week. She's so beautiful that many noble young men want to marry her. You would think she would be very happy but she isn't. She is tired of her life because she thinks it is not useful. After this party she became a nurse. At that time, nurses were often dirty, drunken women. This young girl, with a will of steel, changed all that. She was Florence Nightingale and because of her, nursing became a proud and honourable profession.

Florence Nightingale

The Killer Bees
Are Coming!

Well, at least they are not coming to Japan. But they are coming to Texas from South America. Everybody is very frightened because they attack people very easily. Hundreds of people in Latin America have died from their stings. Anyway, how did they get to America in the first place? In 1957 African killer bees were imported into Brazil for research and experiments. Unfortunately some escaped from the laboratory. Soon they were mixing with the kind and

A killer bee about to attack.

easygoing European bees. Now there are millions of them. They sound like airplanes and are travelling at the rate of 300 miles a year at a height of around 3000 feet.

Soon they will reach Mexico and U.S. Mexican officials hope to trap them there by making them go into bee hives (a bee house) with a special smell. Then they hope to kill

The cat with nine lives.

them by pulling vinyl plastic over the bee hives. Bee experts don't think this will be really successful. Also African killer bees are good hitchhikers! Whole colonies of killer bees together with their queens have travelled on trains from South America to California. And they travelled free without buying tickets! Yes, they are very bad bees.

They say that a cat has nine lives. I think it's true. Many can fall out of a high window and just walk away. They are fine. Mr. Whitney took a cat to the Animal Medical Center in New York. It fell 32 stories (floors) on to a concrete floor. It just walked away practically unharmed! How did it do it? Mr. Whitney thinks that as cats are travelling

The candy of death

through space, they push out their legs, as you can see in the cartoon. When they land, they just relax and push their legs outwards. This softens the landing. They probably learned this technique millions of years ago when they were hunting in high trees.

Why is this piece of candy you see in the cartoon so dangerous? Why can it be sold on the streets for $537 for only one piece? It's because it's made of solid heroin. Heroin is a very expensive and dangerous drug which foolish people take to get excitement. British customs officials found nine kilograms of this 'candy' in the baggage of some people arriving from South Asia. They think there must be some factory in Asia making these 'heroin sweets.' In some parts of Asia heroin is very cheap but in Europe it's very expensive. Bad and evil people make huge profits from these drugs. I'm very happy because

Japan's laws are very strict about any kind of bad drugs. Europe and America have been too soft and easy on drug users so they have many problems.

Is this possible?

Is the scene in this cartoon possible? Is it possible that cavemen hunted dinosaurs and other prehistoric animals? What do YOU think? Anyway, 2,100 students at 41 campuses around America thought that the cavemen did fight dinosaurs. They were wrong. Actually dinosaurs disappeared at least 60 million years before human beings appeared on Earth. Mr. Cronin of U.C.L.A. is worried about science education in these universities. Actually, even Mr. Powle wasn't quite sure about this matter but he knows that supermarkets and ice cream parlours appeared on Earth at the same time as human beings. It's easier than hunting dinosaurs!

Katherine Muzik is a marine biology

The Ishigaki problem

scholar. She is worried about the extension of the airport on Ishigaki Island. She thinks it may destroy a lot of the marine life such as corals and tropical fish. The island is famous for this marine life which is difficult to find in modern times. It is being killed by pollution everywhere. However, the new airport will give jobs to many people and it will increase tourism. This is a very important point too. Perhaps they could build the airport on the west side of the island where most of the coral is already dead. Let's hope they find a solution to this problem.

Who Is the Mystery Boy Who Can't Speak or Hear?

Who is the mystery boy who can't hear, speak or understand anything? No, he's not a poor English Conversation student! In fact, he's a boy about 8 years old who was found by a woman in Juarez, Mexico. At first she thought he was begging for money. So she gave him a thousand pesos. To her surprise he gave the money back to her. He didn't want it. Of course being a deaf-mute who can't hear or speak, he couldn't tell her anything about himself. At first, they thought he was a Mexican boy. Now they think he must be an American because he prefers hamburgers to tacos and enchiladas. He seems to know more about dollars than Mexican pesos and enjoys watching video games. He keeps drawing pictures of an airplane which has crashed with dead bodies all around it. Perhaps he survived an airplane crash. Perhaps he lost his speech and hearing through an airplane accident. Until

He prefers hamburgers to tacos.

someone comes forward and recognizes him, no one will know for certain. Until that time comes, he will remain "the mystery boy of Juarez".

Many farmers now are worried about future imports of American beef and fruits. They wonder whether they can compete against the cheaper agricultural products. However cherry grower Toshio Akatsuka from Yamagata doesn't worry at all. He says he'll think of newer, quicker and better ways to grow cherries. He wants to deliver his delicious cherries straight to the market himself. He wants to have direct relationships with fruit shops. This way he can cut out or avoid the agents and middlemen. His cherries will be fresher, cheaper and be able to compete with American cherries. Akatsuka also wants to break into the big Japanese gift market which Americans don't know about.

Sometimes, as much as ¥2000 is paid for ONE cherry in a gift package! Anyway, I think more farmers should have the same dynamic spirit as Akatsuka. On behalf of consumers and cherry lovers everywhere, I'd like to say, "Congratulations," to Toshio Akatsuka.

What is this? Actually it's a big sculpture of something which looks like a big thumb. It is by a French artist called Cesar and it's being shipped to Seoul for the Olympic Games. Frankly, I don't think it's very beautiful, do you? I suppose I'm a bit foolish because I don't understand a lot of the things they call 'modern art'. Over the FEN radio I heard about one modern American artist. He gets a lady to think up the ideas for his paintings. Then he gets young artists to paint them. He does nothing at all ... except to add his signature and receive millions of

What is this?

Chiyonofuji and 'Rambo'

dollars for 'his' work!

Of course, there's the story of the collector who went to an exhibition of modern art. He stopped before one piece and said, "Wonderful! Look at the strong rectangular shape! Look at the clean, powerful lines. It's simple and yet ... refreshing. I'll buy it." The owner replied, "Yes, it's simple and refreshing. But you can't buy it. It's our air conditioner!"

This is a picture of Sylvester Stallone with Yokozuna Chiyonofuji. Mr. Stallone is better known as 'Rocky' or 'Rambo' to most of his fans. These are the names of the heroes of his movies. He was in Japan to promote his latest action movie 'Rambo III'. Mr. Powle will NOT be seeing this movie because he doesn't like killing, violence and guns. Sumo is a good, clean sport. Mr. Powle prefers Chiyonofuji to 'Rocky' and 'Rambo'!

The Story of Marie Antoinette's Farmhouse

If you go to Europe, you must go to Versailles near Paris. There you will see the most wonderful and luxurious palace in the world. The gardens stretch as far as the eye can see. There are huge fountains and beautiful marble statues. There are beautiful flowers and fruit trees. Then suddenly you see a simple farmhouse. But what is a farmhouse doing in the gardens of such a palace? It has a sad story.

For it was in this very farmhouse 200 years ago that Queen Marie Antoinette used to play with her closest friends. You would think that Marie Antoinette as Queen of France would have had a happy and glamourous life. She did not. She was married at 14 to a fat, boring man. His hobbies were eating, sleeping, hunting and making keys for doors! She didn't like life at the palace either. The royal family had to do everything in public. For example, when the

Her hairstyles got higher and higher.

King and Queen sat down to breakfast, hundreds of people used to come in and watch them. Even when Marie Antoinette had her babies, hundreds of people were watching too!

Soon the beautiful young queen got tired of this life. She spent money like water. She bought diamonds and hundreds of silk dresses. Her hairstyles got higher and higher until they were one metre tall. She used to go gambling and dancing until the early hours of the morning. Her mother, who was the wise and clever Empress of Austria tried to help her daughter through many letters. She wrote, "My ambassador tells me you think only of dancing, dresses and having a good time. You must be more serious or something terrible will happen to you."

Marie Antoinette didn't listen to her mother's wise advice. She suddenly decided she wanted the 'simple life'. It was then that she started to spend a lot of time at Le Hameau or the simple farmhouse. She and her friends used to dress up as shepherds and shepherdesses. The Queen actually used to milk cows herself. Of course the cows were specially cleaned and the milk bowls used by Marie Antoinette were made of expensive Sevres china. Her 'simple' country dresses were made by the best Paris designers. In fact her 'simple' life was more expensive than her life in the palace at Versailles.

In the meantime things were going very badly in France. While Marie Antoinette was playing games with her friends, the people had no food to eat. The French revolution which would change world history was about to begin. France would never be the same again.

At her farmhouse

Once summer afternoon while Marie Antoinette and her friends were at the farmhouse, they hear a terrible noise far away. They stopped milking the cows. They were very afraid. Soon a man came running from the palace. He shouted, "Your Majesty, many hungry and dirty people are coming from Paris. We must hide in the palace or they will kill you."

As Marie Antoinette left she took a last sad look at her private paradise which was the farmhouse. She never saw it again. After that her life was very unhappy. She and the King were forced to go to Paris. The revolution had really begun. They saw that their lives were in danger so they tried to escape. They left Paris in a big coach dressed up as servants. Nobody recognized them so they thought they were safe. The foolish King spent a lot of time eating as usual. Marie Antoinette said, "Hurry up! We are in danger." But the King just replied, "Don't worry. I just want to eat one more chicken." It was that chicken which cost them their lives.

During the journey one man had recognized the King. He looked at the face of the King on a coin. Then he looked at the face of the man who was dressed up as a servant in the big coach. He knew they were the same. Unfortunately he hated the royal family. So he quickly found some soldiers of the revolution who arrested the King and Queen as they were eating. After a terrible journey, they returned to Paris. Soon they were put in prison and condemned to death. In three weeks Marie Antoinette's beautiful golden hair turned snow white with worry for her husband and her children. In prison, even those who used to hate her, could see that she was actually a brave and noble lady.

As she climbed the steps to the guillotine she showed no fear. She seemed to be cold and proud. Perhaps she was
thinking of
happier days when
she was playing
with her friends in
the farmhouse.
You, too, can see
the same farm-
house exactly as

She was cold and proud at the guillotine.

she left it on that terrible summer's day two hundred years ago. Some say that you can see her ghost, dressed up as a shepherdess on hot summer nights. But I don't know about that as I've never seen it myself.

Strange and Interesting Christmas Customs in Britain

At about this time people often ask me, "Is New Year the most important holiday in Britain as it is in Japan?" No, it isn't, Christmas is. In fact, Christmas has been a festival time in Britain for thousands of years. It is supposed to celebrate the birth of Christ but actually he wasn't even born in December. A long time ago a festival lasting from December 21 to December 25 in honour of the Sun God with a lot of eating, drinking and dancing used to take place in Britain. Later this time was used for Christmas.

There's no doubt that when I was a child, Christmas was the most exciting time of the year for me. I used to write a letter to Santa or Father

Worshipping the Sun God at Christmas time.

My father as Santa

Christmas as he's also called, asking for various presents. Then on Christmas Eve, the night before Christmas, I would hang a big stocking at the end of the bed. I'd wake up so excited on Christmas morning. Yes, Santa HAD visited me! The stocking at the end of the bed was full of the presents I had requested...even to the toy model of a Rolls Royce.

Usually, I was so busy opening presents I forgot about time until my mother came in. "Hurry up or we'll be late for church," she would usually say. I never got tired of listening to the Christmas carols in church such as "Silent Night" or "Joy to the World" both of which are now popular in Japan. Sometimes, the priest's talk or sermon was too long. The subject of his sermon would usually be "Are We Forgetting the Real Meaning of Christmas?" In other words, were we

170

thinking too much about presents, eating and drinking and not about religion. Perhaps I was guilty. One time, when his sermon was very long, my deaf grandmother spoke to me in what she thought was a quiet whisper. Actually her voice was very loud and could be heard by everyone in the church. She said, "His sermon is too long. Doesn't he know we're all very hungry? I'm waiting to eat my turkey and Christmas pudding. That's the real meaning of Christmas for ME". Everyone smiled. However, the poor priest's face turned red but he finished his sermon quite quickly after that!

The best part of the Christmas dinner for me was not the turkey but Chistmas pudding. This was because I could find money in it. My mother would get new silver coins such as shillings, sixpences and half crowns. She would boil them for an hour and then put them in the pudding according to an old English custom. It was so exciting to find a silver coin when you bit into the pudding. Once, one of my friends swallowed a silver sixpence by mistake. Everyone was very worried but it came out at the other end in due time!

After dinner, my father would dress up as Santa and he looked quite funny in his red robes. He would then hand out presents from under the Chiristmas tree to everybody. Actually, the Christmas tree is not part of an old British tradition. Queen Victoria's husband, Prince Albert, was German and he brought the Christmas tree custom over from Germany. Soon all British families copied Queen Victoria. Then families all over the world copied British families because Britain was then the most powerful country in the world. Also, about the same time a Londoner started sending cards to all his friends whom he hadn't seen for a long time. And so the Christmas card industry was born.

Kissing under the mistletoe

Another custom we have, is to decorate the house with holly and ivy. It's usually placed over pictures and mirrors. Sometimes, mistletoe is hung from the ceiling. If a man catches a girl standing underneath it, he can kiss her. She can't say, "No" because it's unlucky. Of course, sometimes girls stand under the mistletoe on purpose when they see the right man coming along! This, of course is NOT a Christian custom. It probably dates back to the Druids who were priests in Britain thousands of years ago, long before Christianity. Anyway, even if Christmas is a mixture of both Christian and pagan customs, everyone has a good time . . . and I hope you do too. Merry Christmas and a Happy New Year!

NOTES

葬儀産業の内幕とそこで働く男女の愛を扱った *The Loved One* (1948) は有名。

p. 23　l. 9　**calling a spade a spade**　*American English* のように "*spade*" (鋤) を "*agricultural implement*" (農具) というようなもってまわった言い方はしないといっている。そして *calling a spade a spade* の慣用句 *speak plainly* の意も合わせてかけている。

p. 27　l. 2　**callisthenics** = *calisthenics*　「美容体操」

p. 28　l. 20　**poisonous carbon monoxide gas**　「有毒な一酸化炭素ガス」

p. 29　l. 13　**go on** = *continue saying* (*something*)　「まくしたてる；くどくどといいつのる」ex. *The speaker went on about it.*

p. 31　l. 14　**art**　ここでは「技術」の意で使っている。前述のピカソの *new form of art* (新しい芸術) に対して意味を変転させて，ユーモアを添えている。

p. 33　l. 2　**expert at "buffetmanship"**　「ビュッフェ術を身につけた達人」

　　　l. 18　**somebody is just in front of him about to take**　*be just about to*~ (まさに~しようとする) の構文。誰かがちょうど目前で (残っている1枚のローストビーフを) まさにとろうとする動作を示している。

p. 37　l. 20　**it was not ... Japanese also**　*not only ~ but also* ... (~だけではなく…も) の構文。1週早く来てしまったことに対してだけではなく，自分のおかしな日本語にも聴衆は大笑いしたと述べている。

p. 38　l. 16　**choir** (n.) [kwaiə]　「聖歌隊」

　　　l. 16　**trimming** (n.)　「飾り；余分な装飾」

p. 41　l. 10　**debut** [déibjuː] = make one's first appearance　「デビュー；第一歩」

　　　l. 18　**Genghis Khan style barbecue**　「ジンギスカン式のバーベキュ」*Genghis Khan* (1162~1227) モンゴ

ル帝国の王。モンゴル高原を統一し，1206 年に皇帝となる。その後西夏，満州，イランと東方，西域を治め，世界征服者となった。

| p. 42 | l. 21 | **It wasn't long before . . .** 「ほどなく…しだした；…するにはさほど時間が経過しなかった。」 |

| p. 45 | l. 11 | **avalanche** [ǽvəlæ̀ntʃ] (n.) 「なだれ」 |

| p. 46 | l. 20 | ***"All's well that ends well."*** 「終わりよければすべてよし」シェイクスピアの喜劇の題名をとりこう表現している。1595 年ごろ完成。初演は 1623 年。 |

| p. 48 | l. 14 | **modern Etsuko** *"traditional Etsuko"*（典型的に古い型の *Etsuko*）と対照させている。「今の時代の悦子」を指す。 |

| p. 49 | l. 8 | **counterpart** (n.) 「よく似た人」*modern Etsuko* と対になる，60 年前の古い型の女をここでは指している。 |

| | l. 11 | **laws of supply and demand** 「需要と供給の法則」 |

| p. 51 | l. 10 | **"the role reversal system"** 「役割転倒システム」 女は家事；男は給料をとってくるという従来の役割を逆転させること。 |

| p. 53 | l. 10 | **consumption tax** 「消費税」 |

| p. 54 | l. 16 | **out of curiosity** 「好奇心から」 |

| | l. 26 | **It should be slow and shallow** 坐禅の息使いを説明している。呼吸法は坐禅時の集中力を高める上で重要とされている。 |

| p. 55 | l. 19 | **still and silent figures meditating** 「動かずに心静かに瞑想している人々」 |

| | l. 20 | **I could only see them after a few minutes** 暗い本堂に入ったので目が慣れて瞑想している人が見えるまで，3 分程かかったことを指している。 |

| p. 56 | l. 19 | **Perhaps that is what happened.** 「どうもそれが生じたようだ」*that* は前文で説明したような無の幸わせな境地のことを指している。 |

| p. 57 | l. 2 | **with one throw** 「ひと投げで」一度投げ上げるだけ |

でフトンを上手にたなに上げる日本人の動作を述べ，何度しても失敗した著者との対比を効かせている。

p. 58	l. 11	**My legs seemed to be made of butter.** 長く正座を続けていたので，立ち上がろうとしたとき，足がしっかりしていなく，バターのように柔らかくなり倒れたことを指している。
p. 59	l. 23	**be put off** 「意欲をくじかれる」 ex. *Some pupils are put off learning English by incompetent teaching.*
p. 60	l. 3	**get on the phone**＝*make a phone call* get on（英口語）とりかかる；電話で連絡をつける
p. 61	l. 10	*"Open sesame"* 「ひらけゴマ」*Arabian Night's Entertainment* の中の1つ，*"Ali Baba and the Forty Thieves"* に出てくる開門の呪文。主人公アリババがこの呪文により宝の岩穴に入り，大金持となる。
p. 63	l. 8	**my cold reception** 「私に対する冷たいあしらい」
	l. 25	**In a way I suppose I was** (*a rough and rude foreigner*) ある意味では自分も粗野で粗雑な外人であると思うと，一部肯定している。
p. 65	l. 16	**overcome** (vt.) *surmount; defeat* 「克服する」 ex. *I was still trying to overcome my fear of the dark.*
p. 66	l. 5	**heart failure** 「心不全」
	l. 21	**altitude** (n.) 「(航空機の)高度」
	l. 25	**right** (adv.) *exactly; precisely* 意を強める ex. *Our hotel was right on the beach.*
p. 67	l. 20	**safe** (n.) *a box with thick metal sides and a lock used for protecting valuable things from thieves and fire* 「金庫」
p. 68	l. 5	**burglary** (n.) 「強盗」
p. 70	l. 7	**Yuppies** 「ヤッピィー」本来の *yuppie* の音表語。

young urban professionals の頭文字。専門職を持った都会の青年たちの意。1984年12月31日の "News Week" より使われ始めた言葉。弁護士，医師，証券投資家など30代後半より40代半ばまでのヤングアダルトを指す。

p.71	l.14	**bow . . . wow** 犬のほえ声の音表文字。 cf. ネコのなき声 *meow . . . meow*

l.23　**starving** 「餓死しかけている；ひどく空腹である」ex. *The children were starving after their game of football.*

p.72　l.21　**utilize** (vt.) *make use of; put to some practical use* 「利用する；役立てる」ex. *The cook will utilize the leftover ham bone to make soup.*

p.76　l.23　**break down**=*collapse* ex. *I have seen Virginia break down at rehearsals.*

p.77　l.23　**They say that many . . . buying it.** *They say that many young Japanese girls . . . are buying it.* と解する。

p.78　l.24　**'workaholic'** (n.) 「仕事中毒者」work＋a(lco)-holic cf. *workaholism* (仕事中毒)

p.79　l.7　**floating city** 「海上に浮び建設された都市」

l.11　**Alice** *Lewis Carroll* (1832—98) の Alice's Adventures in Wonderland (1865) の主人公の少女の名。兎の穴からおとぎの国へ行き，種々の冒険をする話。独特の幻想的世界は，現代の詩人・小説家の新しい発想源となり，多大の影響を与えた。

p.81　l.21　**Yukio Mishima** 三島由紀夫 (1925~70) 東京生まれの作家，劇作家。「仮面の告白」(1949) が処女作。「金閣寺」，「宴のあと」，「鹿鳴館」，「憂国」等の作品がある。彼の著作は広く海外に紹介され，川端康成と並び評されることが多い。

p.82　l.17　**work out**=*formulate; produce* 「(話のすじを)練り上げる」ex. *We are always hoping that a* *more peaceful solution can be worked out.*

p. 83 l. 11 **So a few days became a few years.** 石井好子のフランス滞在が，当初の予定の2・3日が，歌手としての契約をしたため，2・3年になってしまったことを述べている。

l. 26 **go by the name of～** 「～さんという名前で知られている」ex. *He went by the alias of Robert Smith for many years.* (彼はロバート・スミスという偽名で何年も知られていた)

p. 84 l. 8 **mining family** 「鉱山で採鉱に従事する家族」cf. *mine* (vt.) 鉱石などを採掘する；石炭などを採るための坑道を掘る

p. 85 l. 5 **take up**＝*engage in; asume* 「(仕事) に就く；着手する」ex. *My assistant left to take up another post.*

p. 86 l. 19 **make part**＝*take part* 「役割を果たす」

p. 87 l. 2 **in a sense** 「ある意味では」

l. 17 **go out of business** 「仕事ができなくなる」*go out of*＝*die out*

p. 88 l. 24 **in the reign of Queen Victoria** 「ヴィクトリア女王の治世に」*Queen Victoria* (1819—1901) の時代，イギリスはインドまで配下に治め，世界的栄華を極めた。

p. 91 l. 14 **get away**＝*start* 「(～の話を) はじめる」

l. 20 **woodblock print** 「木版画」

l. 26 **in her early twenties** 「彼女の二十代前半の頃」cf. *in one's cheerful thirties* 「陽気な三十代」

p. 92 l. 16 **ask for her hand** *ask for one's hand* 「結婚の申し込みをする」

p. 93 l. 7 **risk my life fighting there** 「そこで命がけで戦う」

p. 94 l. 7 **make it**＝*succeed; arrive* (口語)「(首尾よく) やり

179

とげる」ex. *We'll make it with a minute or two to spare.*

p. 96　l. 17　**Not only did . . . to Tokyo!**　「日本のビジネスマンは部屋を出ていっただけでなく、東京に飛んで帰ってしまった」

p. 97　l. 13　**changes for the better**　「改善のための変革」

　　　　l. 21　**at great cost**　「大変な値段で；莫大な金額で」

p. 99　l. 1　**"You are paid to work, not to think."**　「おまえらは考えるためではなく、働くために雇われているのだ」

　　　　l. 20　**in the first place**　「まず最初に」

p. 100　l. 5　**I expect that too will change in time.**　「これもまた、時が解決してくれるであろう」

p. 101　l. 2　**lifemanship**(n.)　「相手より偉いと思わせる術；はったり」

　　　　l. 16　**one-up** (a.)　「一枚うわての；一段優位に立った」

　　　　l. 21　**lifeman** (n.)　「*lifemanship* を用いる人」

p. 104　l. 22　**is usually never at a loss for words**　「通常、決して言葉に窮することにならない」

p. 106　l. 1　**public school**　「パブリックスクール」イギリスのパブリックスクールは、*public* といっても公立ではない。上・中流子弟のための寄宿制の私立中等学校のこと。イートン、ハロー、ラグビィーなどのパブリックスクールは有名。

　　　　l. 5　**private school**　「私立学校」

　　　　l. 13　**charter** (n.)　「設立許可(書)」

p. 107　l. 7　**class distinction**　「階級差別」

　　　　l. 11　**'snob'**　「スノッブ」ここでは階級が低く貧しいのに、知的教養を身につけた紳士気取りの人間を指している。普通は俗物紳士や、知ったかぶりをする俗人をいう。

p. 108　l. 12　**cockney accent**　「ロンドンなまり；コクニーなまり」語尾の [h] を発音しなかったり、[ei] を [ai] と発音したりする。このコクニーなまりを矯正し、レディに仕

180

立て上げる *My Fair Lady* の話は有名。

をつけて潜水すること。*scuba* とは <u>*self-contained*</u> <u>*under water breathing apparatus*</u> の頭文字。圧搾空気のシリンダーと、目と鼻につけるマスクを含む潜水用水中呼吸器を指す。

l. 20　**Maybe the dinner prices . . . in Tokyo!**　著者の行った *Borocay Island* での食事料金は、マニラの半分、東京の5分の1という、物価の比較をしている。

p. 123　l. 5　**get on to the subject** ＝ *change to the subject during conversation*　「話題を向ける」ex. *That's something we'll get on to in the future.*

p. 124　l. 18　**it's like Cinderella's ugly sister**　著者が小さくきゅうくつなウェットスーツを無理やり着ようとする姿は、シンデレラが落していった靴を手がかりに、ピタリとはける人を探す際の、無理にもはいてしまおうとする余り美しくない姉の姿に似ていることを指している。

l. 24　**fit out** ＝ *equipt*　「装備する」

p. 126　l. 23　**And just the fact . . . a fantasy.**　*the fact . . . is like a fantasy* と解する。

p. 128　l. 5　**why not try** ＝ *please try*　*why not* ＋動詞の原形で提案（*suggestion*）の意で使う。ex. *Why not study hard?*

l. 8　**Antarctic** (a.)「南極の」cf. *arctic* (南極の) *anti* ＋ *arctic* より。

p. 129　l. 13　**trek** (n.) （アフリカ南部）「牛車にのって旅行すること」

p. 130　l. 26　**London via Moscow**　「モスクワ経由でロンドン」*via* ＝ *by way of*　「～経由で」ex. *She travelled from Dover to Edinburgh via London.*

p. 132　l. 6　**not as problems but as adventures**　*not ～ but . . .* の構文。(～ではなく…)「困ったこととしてではなく、冒険として（それらを考えなさい）」

l. 22　**make one's way to～**　「～へと向かう」

p. 133	l. 14	**by slow stages** 「休み休み，ゆっくり(旅して)」ex. *We travelled by slow (easy) stages, stopping often along the way.*

p. 133　l. 14　**by slow stages** 「休み休み，ゆっくり(旅して)」ex. *We travelled by slow (easy) stages, stopping often along the way.*

p. 134　l. 10　**to be addressed** 「話しかけられること」 *address* (vt.) *cause oneself to begin to speak to a person*「人に話しかける」ex. *I was addressed by a stranger.*

p. 135　l. 11　**It might be in one hour but it might be one day.** 「1時間かもしれないし，また1日かかるかもしれない」

p. 136　l. 5　**that strange black stuff** 「あの見慣れぬ奇妙な黒いもの」 *stuff* (n.) *things in a mass; matter* ex. *The meat is good stuff.*

p. 137　l. 12　**had to share with another** 「他の人と同室しなければならない。」

　　　　l. 26　**KGB** ロシア語の *Komitet Gosudarstvennoi Bezopasnosti* の略。「ソ連国家保安委員会」(*Committee of State Security*)

p. 138　l. 6　**bug** (vt.) (口語)「〜に隠し盗聴マイクを備える」

　　　　l. 15　**put someone off 〜ing** *put off＝discourage* (*someone*) *from 〜* ex. *The smell put me off eating a week.*

p. 139　l. 5　**apart from**＝*except for; without considering* 「(〜を)のぞいて；別にして」ex. *She had no money, apart from the five pounds that he had given her.*

　　　　l. 19　**ex-President** 「前大統領」 *ex-* は官名などの前に付いて *former* (以前の) の意を表わす。ex. *ex-premier／ex-husband*

p. 140　l. 16　**front row seat** 大相撲の観覧席で，土俵に一番近い，「砂かぶり」といわれる席。*row* (n.)「列，行」ex. *a row of trees* (並木)／*in three rows* (3列になって)

p. 141　l. 15　**'spice it up'**　「それに面白味を添える」*spice* (vt.)
「〜に味を添える，趣をこらす」

p. 144　l. 9　**afford** (vt.) *be able to buy*　ex. *At last, we can afford a house.*

p. 145　l. 10　**in disguise with ~**　「〜で変装して」*disguise* (n.)「変装；ごまかし」

　　　l. 23　**Her husband had left her and taken her two daughters with him.**　彼女を残して夫は去ったが，二人の娘を連れていったことを指す。

p. 147　l. 11　**take a bus**　『バスに乗る』"*take a bus*" を "*take a bath*" (お風呂に入る) のように発音されたため，聞き違えたおかしみを語っている。

　　　l. 14　**globe** (n.)　「天体」特に *the＋globe* で地球の意。

　　　l. 25　**soap not soup**　*soap* [sóup|sóup]，soup [súːp] のように発音が違うが，誤った発音により混乱がおきた。

p. 149　l. 9　**If you do this, your unhappiness will actually make you stronger.**　あなたがそれ（まず失敗しても，何度も何度も試みてみること）をすれば，そうした不幸が実際にあなたをより強くするということ。

p. 150　l. 7　**dark-eyed lady**　「黒い瞳の女性」*one-eyed Jack* (片目のジャック)，*blue-eyed Mary*(青い眼のメアリー)

　　　l. 12　**William Shakespeare** (1564—1616)　「ウィリアム・シェイクスピア」イギリスの詩人・劇作家。ここで述べられている *Dark Lady* は，彼のソネットの中で讃われている女性。正体はまだ不明とされている。

p. 151　l. 3　**Sir Winston Churchill** (1874〜1965)　英国の政治家。1900 年保守党員として下院議員となったが，保護関税に反対し自由党に転じ，その後 1924 年保守党に復帰。1940 年保守党党主となり 1945 年まで首相。1951 年再度首相となり 1955 年辞任。文筆家，雄弁家として知られ絵筆もとった。1953 年「第二次大戦回顧録」でノーベル文学賞受賞。

l. 17 **Adolf Hitler**（1889〜1945）　ドイツの政治家。オーストリア出身。1921 年ナチ党の指導権を握る。反ユダヤ主義とゲルマン民族の優越性を主張。近隣諸国を次々に侵略し、第二次世界大戦を引き起す。ベルリン陥落直前、官邸で自殺した。

p. 152　l. 18 **Vincent Van Gogh**（1853〜90）　オランダの画家。ゴッホはアルル、パリ周辺の風景、自画像等を、強烈な色彩により描いた。狂気のうちに自殺した。

p. 153　l. 8 **Florence Nightingale**（1820〜1910）　英国の看護婦。野戦病院で活躍した後、ナイチンゲール・ホーム等の病院、施設の改善に務め、近代的看護技術の開拓者となった。

p. 155　l. 19 **a cat has nine lives**　「猫には命が九つある（叩いたくらいではなかなか死なない）」のことわざより。cf. *Care killed the cat*.なかなか死なない九生ある猫をも心配が殺した（心配は身の毒）

p. 156　l. 19 **customs**（n.）*import duties*　「関税；税関」cf. *custom office*（税関事務所）

p. 157　l. 12 **caveman**（n.）= *cave dweller*「（ヨーロッパ旧石器時代の）洞窟に住んだ人」

　　　　l. 26 **marine biology scholar**　「海洋生物学の学者」cf. *marine biology* 海洋生物学

p. 159　l. 9 **peso**（n.）「ペソ」メキシコ、キューバ、アルゼンチン、チリ、コロンビアなどの通貨単位。

　　　　l. 16 **enchilada** [èntʃəláːdə]（n.）「エンチラーダ」とうがらし（チリ）をきかせて調味した肉や野菜を詰めたトルティーヤのようなもの。

p. 162　l. 11 **rectangular shape**　「長方形のかたち」

　　　　l. 16 **Sylvester Stallone**（1946〜　）　ニューヨーク生まれの男優。1975 年偶然見たボクシングの試合に感動し、「ロッキー」の脚本を書く。映画化され世界的にヒットとなり、スターの座を築く。「ロッキー」「ランボー」共にシリーズ化され、いずれもヒットしている。

p. 163　l. 14　**Queen Marie Antoinette**（1755～93）　フランス王ルイ十六世の王妃，マリー・アントワネット。オーストリア大公・ハンガリーの女王であるマリア・テレジアの娘。民衆蔑視により国民の反感を招いた。フランス革命により1793年処刑された。

p. 165　l. 8　**Sevres china**　「セーブル焼きの陶磁器」*Sevres* フランスのパリ郊外にあるセーヌ河畔の都市。陶磁器の産地。

　　　　l. 16　**The French Revolution**　「フランス革命」18世紀末のフランスの市民革命。自由・平等・博愛を求め，1789年7月バスチーユの監獄の襲撃に始まり，1799年ナポレオンの権力獲得をもって終わった。

p. 167　l. 15　**guillotine**（n.）　「ギロチン」1789年フランスの医師 *J.I. Guillotin*（1738～1814）が提案した首切りの刑具の名。大きな刃が上から落ちてきて，さしのべられている首が落ちる仕掛け。

p. 172　l. 24　**holly and ivy**　「赤い実のついたヒイラギとアイビー」
p. 173　l. 1　**mistletoe**（n.）　「ヤドリギ」
　　　　l. 8　**Druids**（n.）　「ドルイド」古代ケルト族の間に行なわれたドルイド教の祭司。予言者，詩人，裁判官なども務めた指導的知識階級。信仰の内容は太陽崇拝，霊魂不滅を中心思想とする土俗的なもの。キリスト教の伝来により滅びた。

【注：井上美沙子（大妻女子大学教授）】

My Humorous Japan

| 発行日 | 1991(平成3)年12月20日　第1刷発行 |
| | 2005(平成17)年8月5日　第38刷発行 |

著　者　ブライアン W. ポール

発行者　大橋晴夫

発行所　日本放送出版協会
　　　　東京都渋谷区宇田川町41-1
　　　　郵便番号150-8081
　　　　電話番号03-3780-3308(編集)・03-3780-3339(販売)
　　　　http://www.nhk-book.co.jp
　　　　振替　00110-1-49701

装　幀　柿崎　寿
印　刷　啓文堂／大熊整美堂
製　本　田中製本
Printed in Japan
ISBN4-14-035032-6 C0082